JAILBREAK
LEADERSHIP

FREE YOUR PURPOSE
DISCOVER YOUR CALLING
LIVE AND LEAD WITH
MEANING AND IMPACT

JEFF BLANTON

Larry
Thanks for
all of your
support

Jailbreak Leadership
Published by Telltale Publishing
Copyright © 2017 by Jeff Blanton
All rights reserved.

Telltale Publishing
A Division of Blanton Group, Inc.
4457 Mission Blvd., Suite 201
San Diego, CA 92109
Email: info@blantongroup.com

Limit of Liability/Disclaimer of Warranty:

Publishing and editorial team:
Author Bridge Media, www.AuthorBridgeMedia.com
Project Manager and Editorial Director: Helen Chang
Editor: Katherine MacKenett
Publishing Manager: Laurie Aranda
Publishing Assistant: Iris Sasing
Cover Design: Terri Podlenski, Smart Creative Lab, Inc.

Library of Congress Control Number: 2017913134

ISBN: 978-0-9992886-0-3 -- softcover
978-0-9992886-1-0 -- ebook

Ordering Information:

Quantity sales. Special discounts are available on quantity purchases by corporations, associations, and others. For details, contact the publisher at the address above.

Printed in the United States of America

CONTENTS

ACKNOWLEDGMENTS

I would like to offer special thanks to my wife, Caryn Blanton, who not only supported my personal journey of discovering and living a purposeful life but also has been such a great example of "walking the talk" in her own life. She has shown me why others need to know and act on their purpose. If not for her, I would still be in "jail" with my smoldering discontent and agitation, craving something more.

I also want to thank my great friend and confidant Rob Shimizu. Rob was the devil's advocate for me in pulling together this project, and he challenged all of my beliefs every step of the way—all the while making me feel highly supported and valued, even when I managed to drive golf balls at parked cars and the clubhouse at his home golf course.

I also want to thank a host of folks who helped to translate my nonsense into English, starting with Katherine MacKenett from Author Bridge Media. She heard beyond the words on the paper to my true message and helped me deliver on their meaning clearly and succinctly. I also want to thank Dan Cooper, Neil Trevisan, and

Keturah Kennedy for their time and effort in reading the manuscript and providing great feedback and insight.

A special thanks to all my "beta projects"—the individuals who were willing to be the subjects of my experimental "jailbreak" process until I finally figured it out, especially Mikkele Hill, Matt Sauer, and Barry Sappington. Thank you to those early adopters who just kept coming back. I am also grateful to Angie Knierman, Jared Kelly, Mike Gaetke, Chris Francis, and Jennifer Krewalk.

And finally, I'd like to thank my marketing guru, Terri Podlenski, who has helped me to take both the book and the Jailbreak Leadership process beyond the four walls of my office, so that it can make an impact in the world.

INTRODUCTION

Behind Bars

Is there anything more tragic than an innocent person getting thrown in jail?

Think about that for a second. You're just ambling along, living an honest life. Your biggest interface with the judicial system is most likely a traffic ticket. You have no reason to be overly concerned about false incarceration. You follow the rules, pay your taxes, and attempt to live a life of integrity.

Then, out of nowhere—*bam!* Handcuffs. Someone in a blue uniform shoves you into the back of a police car. Before you know what's happening, you've been convicted of a crime you didn't commit. And the next thing you know, you're in jail. Trapped. Behind bars.

If you're thinking, "That could never happen to me," I have some news for you. It already has.

In fact, it started a very long time ago—when you were about two years old, if you want to get specific. Remember the "terrible twos"? That was the first time you started to express your wants and desires to the world. What response did you receive from your parents? Something like "You cannot have or do everything you want!" Right? Maybe it even came with a little thump to the side of your head or a whack to your backside.

Thus it begins. This is your first step into incarceration: your expectations of who you are and what you should be doing in life, as set by others. Your success as defined by an endless loop of chasing after more and more power, prestige, and position.

You have played this game for years. And the result is that you're coming up short—both as a leader in your organization and in your personal goals.

At your company, you feel stuck in this constant grind to just maintain. Any incremental joy associated with success is fleeting at best, with just one more problem to solve always riding on its heels. Where is all the meaning and impact you envisioned when starting this venture or career?

And it's not just you. Your employees are consistently uninspired too—just listless robots showing up to turn the crank every day. Worse, you feel powerless to change that, because if you're being honest, you know how they feel.

Truth be told, you drank the Kool-Aid. You bought the story hook, line, and sinker that success would bring peace and joy into your life. Instead, you're strapped down in this monotonous machine, smoldering with discontent—knowing that tomorrow will be just one more day in a long line of nearly identical days.

Maybe this assessment by author Nigel Marsh describes your situation: "There are thousands and thousands of people out there living lives of quiet, screaming desperation, where they work long, hard hours at jobs they hate to enable them to buy things they don't need to impress people they don't like."

Or maybe you're one step beyond that, and philosopher Ravi Zacharias is your man. He said, "The loneliest moment in life is when you have just experienced that which you thought would deliver the ultimate, and it just let you down."

Whatever the case, everything you've been through as a leader and as a person has left you with one very important question: *Is this it?*

And somewhere inside you, you already sense the answer: *No.*

In your gut, you know there's a larger world beyond this prison. There's a grander purpose for your organization, your life, and your journey. You can feel it in your bones. You're hungry to make the bigger impact you know you're capable of making. But you're locked behind bars you can't even see. And the longer you stew in confinement, the more another question begins to gnaw at you:

Is there a way out?

The Great Escape

The bars of your invisible prison have been confining you all your life. But here's some good news.

Once you know what they are and how to deal with them, you can stage a prison break.

Breaking out of prison gets you one sweet, simple reward: freedom. The freedom to be YOU! The freedom to do what you are designed to do—to finally throw off the constraints that have been laid on you, so that you can fully pursue the kind of life and leadership role that you have always felt called to. The freedom to know unequivocally—and to act on—your purpose in this life.

No more guesswork. No more doubts. Once you bust out of prison, you can just *go out and do it!*

And the best news of all is this: you already have everything you need to break free. Your personal escape plan is a gift that's already been delivered to you. Your only job is to receive it, open the package, see what you have been given to work with, and put it into action.

When you do, leadership—and life—starts to look a whole lot different.

Imagine: What would it look like to be the Michael Jordan of your particular niche in the world? How would you feel at the end of a day when you spent 90 percent of your time doing what you loved to do versus an industry standard of 20 percent? How would it feel to shift from the endless striving for "success" to creating a legacy of significance?

This is not just about a bigger, better career. This is about bringing significance to all aspects of your life. There is no need to pretend or keep up with the Joneses anymore.

You now have the opportunity to fully embrace who you are.

You don't have to settle for the status quo. You can lead with unconstrained vision, fueled by a purpose that both drives you and makes a greater impact in the world than you ever thought possible.

But to get there, you're going to have to orchestrate the biggest jailbreak of your life. And that's where having an escape plan comes in.

My First Prison Break

Breaking out of prison isn't easy—but it is worth it. I know, because I'm a longtime fugitive myself.

I first broke out of prison in my thirties. Granted, at the time, it wasn't exactly by choice.

You've probably heard the line "It's all about hard work." My parents were very hardworking individuals. The mantra around our house was "Do the work, and if it's not working out, then just work harder." They themselves had bought into this belief, and they passed it along to me.

Following this advice, I rose to a second-level management position in a midsized medical-device company. I had taken over a group that had been struggling, and after about a year and a half, I was feeling pretty proud of the progress we were making.

Outside my sphere of influence, major changes were happening, including a change of ownership in the company. My boss threw me a "hint" that I might be in trouble because of the shakeup, but I didn't pay much attention. I was sure it wouldn't affect me. I already worked harder than most anyone I knew. During the company's big transition, I just doubled down on my efforts, checking off even more boxes, making more improvements, and hitting all the department's milestones.

Then came the fateful day of the corporate-wide layoff.

As individuals were escorted out of the building, my executive assistant came in and told me, "Don't worry; you're not on the list." I was surprised she thought I needed to know that. I didn't have any worries about being on the list. But it turned out there must have been another list.

In the words of my boss at the time: "You're now the third director reporting to me, and I only need one. You're not it."

Being laid off rocked me like I'd been punched. In the

space of a single day, my lifelong belief that hard work was the answer crumbled beneath my feet.

Now don't get me wrong; it's tough to get somewhere in this world without doing the work. But it's not *always* about hard work. Sometimes we just need to stop, pull our heads out of the sand, and pay attention to what the heck is going on.

Was it fun to get my butt thrown out into the street? Not exactly. But with the walls of my prison stripped away, I had plenty of time to figure out how I'd been jailed all those years without knowing it. I realized just how many times I'd missed the real opportunities in my life while I was so busy working hard—and how many opportunities were available to me now that I had a new view of things.

After that, I started breaking myself out of jail on purpose. And that was when real success started to make an appearance in my life.

Escape Artist

As a business leader myself, I have always been passionate about vision and mission.

I was very fortunate early in my career to recognize that my leadership strength lay in spearheading small-to-big teams and helping them create new futures for themselves. Regardless of how half-baked an organization's vision might be, the initiative that would usher in its new tomorrow always warranted its own purpose for being—whether it was a new product, consolidating large facilities for survival, driving major organizational culture change, or even launching a new company altogether.

In every case, I could shift the group's sight away from the bean-counter bottom-line goal and toward a compelling vision of the impact this initiative would make on the company, its customers, and its employees. People need meaning to fuel them—especially when they're venturing into the unknown and trying to survive gut-wrenching challenges. I was the guy who brought the spark plug, the passion, and the courage to make it happen.

I have successfully executed hundreds of projects around the world in all kinds of situations with consistent success—in an environment where 80 percent failure is the norm. In the process, I have learned that beyond the business purpose we could all see on the surface lay a multitude of other goals and purposes: those that belonged to the individuals involved in the bigger project.

My real job, I realized, was to help people identify those individual desires so that they could then bring their full force toward achieving the collective goal of the business. This was the catalyst for creating the energy, commitment, and conviction to drive a project's success even in the most difficult environments. It became my personal secret sauce that never failed.

Now I'm sharing the recipe.

Jailbreak Leadership is a new way of approaching how you lead your business. Our movement is just getting started, but the individuals who have done this work are already finding a whole new passion for what they do and how they lead—one that is bringing them clarity and allowing them to confidently make important decisions that are in line with who they are.

For those willing to embrace the process and do the work, Jailbreak Leadership is a game changer. Most self-help processes are about getting better. Your whole life has been spent trying to get better in order to meet someone else's expectations. But being a Jailbreak Leader is about having the freedom to know, embrace, and lead your business as the real you.

Getting there is a tall order. But if you've never staged a prison break before, don't panic. Just stay close on my tail. Together, we'll get you to the freedom that's waiting for you on the other side. That is my commitment to you.

The Plan

This book is not a novel. While reading it should be interesting (and, I hope, somewhat entertaining), it will not influence your life unless you are willing to do the work suggested in these chapters.

Doing the work as you read isn't always easy. I myself am the worst when it comes to this. I'll read a book with every intention to go back and do the work later, and guess what? It never happens. That's my loss, every time it happens.

So to get the most out of this book, you have to be more than a reader. You have to be a seeker.

Seekers are individuals who have come to a place in their lives where their beliefs do not answer their questions anymore. They realize that their worldviews are wrong, and they are willing to seek the truth until they find it. Seekers are ready and willing to engage, embrace change, and do the required work to get what they want.

Even though I sometimes flake out when I'm reading on my own, I have personally had great success working through books like this with my wife. Accountability helps. Having someone who already sees the greatness in you that you still need to reveal helps too. Surrounding yourself with people like this during the discovery process, while you take action and, quite honestly, for the rest of your life, is the most powerful way to become a Jailbreak Leader.

If you're not sure who those people are, don't let it stop you. My team and I are always here to support seekers in their jailbreaks and on their journeys. Just give us a holler at info@jailbreakleadership.com, and we'll get you there.

Freedom Calling

Only 1/10 of 1 percent of inmates ever escape from prison, according to the Bureau of Justice Statistics. The scary thing is that percentage holds true for the rest of us in our personal prisons as well.

Everyone is born with an innate desire to know the meaning of life. Why are we here? Few will take the time to pursue this question. The rest will fill the gap with being busy. Even among the few leaders who take the time to gain the knowledge of what it all means, most will then sit on the wall of indecision and never take action.

And then there are the elite leaders. These are the few who truly desire to lead change, and to have a significant impact, not just for themselves but for others. They hear freedom calling, and they're willing to do whatever it takes to turn the knowledge of what they're here to do into action.

If you're one of the elite, welcome to the team. It's going to be a wild ride—one that you won't soon forget. Escape starts with you—with a willingness to go against the grain. Are you ready to join the ranks of Jailbreak Leaders transforming lives across the globe?

You are? Great.

Then let's bust out of this joint.

Chapter 1

The Prison System

*The place God calls you to is the place where your
deep gladness and the world's deep hunger meet.*

—*Frederick Buechner,*
Wishful Thinking: A Theological ABC

Why the Struggle?

Have you ever watched the reality TV show *COPS*?

If not, here's the premise. An individual, usually ine-
briated, has captured the attention of local law enforcement. Regardless of whatever discussion, chases, or
crashes occur in the first fourteen minutes of the segment,
the ending is always the same. A small army of the city's
finest, with much fanfare, struggle, moaning, and groan-
ing, will finally smash the struggling perp to the ground
and slap on the handcuffs.

I never fully understood why every arrest ended in a
struggle until many years ago, when I had my very own
COPS moment. (Please note, I said, "Many years ago!")

Like my friends on *COPS*, I admit there was some alcohol involved. By all accounts, it had been a good evening with the gang at our local hot spot. Last call had come and gone, and we were heading to my buddy's car. The club was only about ten minutes from my home, but in all my youthful wisdom, it seemed like a good idea to go up into the bushes next to the bank building to relieve myself.

I know, I know, but come on. We've all been there!

Next thing I know, I have a bright spotlight shining on me from a patrol car.

Because all my mental imaging about what to do in a crisis situation like this came from lying on the couch watching *COPS*, I began doing my best forty-yard dash across the parking lot. But after a quick scan of my surroundings revealed a twelve-foot wall and two more cruisers heading my way to block off my escape route, I recognized the futility of my actions.

I came to a screeching halt in the middle of the parking lot. Hands in the air, just like on TV, I yelled, "I give up!"

Of course, within seconds of my surrender, a very large and heroic police officer brought this crime spree fully under control with a flying tackle. Taking no chances, he then secured my face into the asphalt with his knee, as a crowd of his associates slapped the infamous cuffs on my wrists.

I don't condone this type of book research. However, I now know the answer to the question "Why the struggle?"

The answer is simple: freedom.

The Prison System

We all crave freedom. Regardless of the crazy circumstances, and no matter how drunk or drugged, any criminal instinctively knows that freedom is worth fighting for. Once those handcuffs appear, you know your freedom is about to go away. As humans, it's in our DNA—and our belief in God-given rights, the land of the free, and all that—to put up a fight. We want to be able to do what we want to do when we want to do it. The idea of being incarcerated and controlled by the system goes completely against everything we know to be true.

Like it or not, though, we are all born into a prison system.

This structure of incarceration is so subtle, unfailing, and holistic that most of us don't even know we're in jail. Our prison system is not a jail of metal bars and stone-faced guards, but a prison of the mind—one that slowly closes around us, taking our freedom. Ultimately, the results are the same as for those put into a physical prison.

And the worst part? Nobody in our society is an exception to the rule.

This isn't a question of *if* you're in jail.

It's a question of how incarcerated you've become.

This is a very serious matter. Your jail is the context from which you operate. How you lead, how you live, how your relationships are formed, your thoughts on health, and even your faith are determined by the constraints of the jail of your mind.

Don't believe this applies to you? Finish this sentence: I am too _____ (old, young, dumb, busy, poor, etc.) to what? What dreams, hopes, or ideas are completely incarcerated by the constraints of the jail of your mind?

No one is immune to the prison system. No one is blessed with a "Get out of jail free" card. And it's been this way for a long time.

Freedom Is a Choice

People have lived in the "jail" of expectations imposed on them by society and authority since the beginning of civilization. Even as recently as one or two generations ago, right here in America, life was very predictable and defined. Individuals typically had a career with one company, bought the house, had the kids, and, if their luck held out, retired at sixty-five. Then, if they had anything left over, they enjoyed a few years of retirement before cashing out.

But we are blessed to live in an extraordinary time and place, and this pattern has changed in recent history.

The success and power of the baby-boom generation, the pace of change, the effects of globalization, the new experience of having multiple careers, and the increased life span of humans as a whole have challenged our views of the world—and opened our eyes to an expanded vision of what could be.

The catch is that, even though we have been given greater opportunity to explore and dream than at any other time in history, our jailers have upped their game too.

Society has come up with some pretty sophisticated ways to keep us locked in place. We live in a world of selfies, comparisons, and "look at me" social media—things that keep us so self-absorbed that we don't even think to look beyond the bars of our prisons. Our materialistic idea of success consumes our attention and energy as we keep charging around the hamster wheel, scrambling to get our piece of the pie and often, in the process, becoming more and more incarcerated through credit and debt.

Most insidious of all, we've come to think of our prisons themselves as "not such a bad place to be." As Timothy Ferriss, author of *The 4-Hour Workweek*, states, "Most people will choose unhappiness over uncertainty."

Each and every one of us has the ability to ask the questions that can set us free. The question is, are you willing to leave the comfort of your cell to chase the adventure of what could be—to an adventure that shifts your thinking from success to significance, from "more for me" to "what can I offer?"

Every American generation from the baby boomers onward has been given the option to be free. But freedom is a choice. And it's a choice that most are not willing to make. The constraints, the powers that be, and our own fear of the unknown keep most of us securely in place.

But for those willing to lead a jailbreak, the opportunity is here. And for Jailbreak Leaders, the biggest significance they will bring to the world is not what they will achieve, but the opportunity they will provide for others to discover true freedom.

You can be one of them.

Breakout

It takes an exceptional person to escape our "prison system." But some leaders do break out. Odds are, you know some of the more famous ones: Elon Musk. Steve Jobs. Oprah Winfrey. Richard Branson. Sheryl Sandberg. Warren Buffet . . . just to name a few.

These people live bigger lives. They have found a way to operate outside of the prison system and to unleash the leadership that has literally changed—and continues to change—the world.

When you choose to become a Jailbreak Leader, guess

what? This is the party you're inviting yourself to. You're smashing through the status quo and entering a space of uncharted waters—and untapped possibility. You're choosing to play a bigger game. And on a playing field this size, your potential to make an impact becomes limitless.

The challenge is this: How do you get from mental incarceration to unlimited freedom?

You do it by recognizing and understanding the prison system you're in—by mapping it out like a true escape artist, breaking loose, and then taking steps to remain a fugitive for the rest of your life.

Is this an easy task? No. But can it be done?

Absolutely.

Your Escape Plan

This book is designed to help you break out of jail—permanently.

If you desire the freedom to lead with unconstrained vision, strategy, and execution—all based on the context of your personal purpose—you're going to have to pull off a jailbreak escape. To do it successfully, we're going to build you a personalized escape plan in five steps.

1. **Jail.** Prison looks a little different for everybody. Yours is tailor-made to fit you. Before you can break out of jail, you need to identify

what put you behind bars to begin with. Understanding this starts with a self-assessment of your incarceration. When you recognize where you are, you can figure out where you want to escape to.

2. **The Key.** Your personal key that lets you out of jail is built on three things: your power, your principles, and your purpose. Once you have the "3P Key" of self-knowledge, you can open your cell door to freedom.

3. **The Call.** Escaping prison is not for the faint of heart. To pull it off, your conviction in what you're doing needs to be greater than your fear of breaking out—not to mention more compelling than the comfort of your familiar jail cell. Identifying your call and the vision of what you want to achieve will keep you driving forward as you scale the walls.

4. **Jailbreak.** You are the sum of your choices, and your choices are the result of your habits. To finally break out of your mental prison, you need to do the hard work of changing yourself by changing your habits. Once you do, you can use your new perspective to anticipate challenges and fight your way to freedom.

5. **Fugitive.** Even after they escape, about 92 percent of prisoners get captured and thrown back in jail. To be one of the 8 percent who keep their freedom, you have to stay vigilant, keeping yourself purpose driven and accountable every day that you're at large. This is where you really gain the power to transform your life and your business.

The night I lost my freedom was embarrassing (although "resisting arrest" sounds way better than "peeing in the bushes"). I spent the night in jail and caused myself a fair amount of stress.

But I knew my situation. I understood the rules that were broken, and, with a big chunk of money, I could fight the good fight. In the end, the judge assigned to my case said, without mincing any words, "You are an idiot! Grow up, and never come back to my court again."

And I was free.

The road to freedom can be hard going. Even when you understand the prison system inside and out, you sometimes still have to face off against a lot of barbed wire or dark, underground sewer routes before you reach the world beyond the fence.

Here's the thing, though. The fight for freedom is always worth it.

And it begins with knowing your own prison.

Chapter 2

Jail

To be yourself in a world that is constantly trying to make you something else is the greatest accomplishment.

—*Ralph Waldo Emerson*

By the Numbers

The number of innocent people thrown in jail each year is staggering.

In 2014 and 2015 alone, the United States absolved more than three hundred people of the wrongdoings they'd been imprisoned for. Many of those exonerated were on death row or serving life without parole.

And that's just the high-profile cases. If the system is making those kinds of mistakes at that level, can you imagine what's happening to the thousands of people who go through the lower courts? According to the documentary *13th*, 97 percent of the more than two million individuals currently incarcerated never had a trial.

In other words, it's impossible to know the actual number of falsely imprisoned individuals—but estimates are in the tens of thousands.

And as tragic as that sounds, those numbers have nothing on the prison system that's incarcerating the rest of us.

Jail

We're all in mental jail. All 314 million of us. We can't help it. It's part of the equation.

But that doesn't mean we have to accept it.

Escape begins with mapping out your personal prison by figuring out which beliefs and limitations have been holding you captive all these years. All of us have a worldview based on the beliefs that we have collected over the course of our lives. When you want to initiate change and get a different outcome, you have to start by challenging that worldview and the beliefs behind it.

It is critical to know what you are up against. If you take the time to figure out what's holding you back before you start fighting it, you can land punches that hit the target instead of wasting time flailing around in the dark. Identifying the equation is the fastest way to solve it— and understanding your worldview is the fastest way out of your mental prison.

I myself was a little slow to catch on to this.

If you asked me what I did for a living just a few years ago, I would have said, "Strategy execution." Basically, I parachuted into companies and turned their big strategic initiatives around for them. In my world of execution, I had two nemeses: quality and regulatory people (who loved to tell me what I could *not* do but never brought along a solution for what we *could* do), and creative types. Man, those creatives drove me nuts. They had great ideas, but they always fell short when it came to actually getting something done.

So I was shocked and a bit offended one day when my wife commented, "You are a creative." She had thrown me into my enemy's camp! I was sure she must be wrong.

But then I started mapping out my prison. Turns out, I really am very creative. One self-awareness test I took puts people into one or two major categories out of five—and one of the five categories is for people high on "execution." Nothing about me fell into the execution category. In fact, if you really want to kill me, give me a daily operations position.

That's right—I was sentenced to forty years in a career where a good 90 percent of my strengths were misplaced. And having clarity about this one significant piece of my jail was profound. In the space of two years, I used that knowledge to put myself where I really belonged: helping other people break out of prison.

When it comes to breaking out of your mental prison,

you first need to understand the challenge itself. What are you up against? There are thousands of things that could be keeping you where you are.

This chapter will cover the many common ways in which we are "shackled" by the world around us and will walk you through the process of mapping your personal prison, so that you can plot your great escape.

The Shackles of Society

You have been the victim of an elaborate con—and probably more than one of them. The worst part is that, all these years, you've been making major life-altering decisions based on information that's full of half-truths and outright lies.

Being trapped by the shackles of society doesn't have much in common with *COPS*. There's no car chase, no sprint across the parking lot, and no big final tussle to the ground. Instead, it's just an endless, unfulfilling, submissive perp walk through life.

The first step to unlocking those shackles is understanding how you've been locked up.

When it comes to identifying our personal prisons, most of us find ourselves restrained by six common types of "cuffs": community, circumstances, complicity, possessions, authority, and systems.

Cuffs of Community

I define *community* as the people around you: parents, friends, teachers, employees, customers, mentors, neighbors, your local mail carrier—anyone in your vicinity whom you have contact with is part of your community. The beliefs we pick up from this group of people are usually some of the earliest things that put us—and then keep us—in jail.

Now it's probably safe to say that most of the people in your community want the best for you. Nevertheless, when you begin piecing together all the little lies, half-truths, well-intentioned protective opinions, and philosophies from the people who know and care about you, you quickly start to see that there might be a programming problem.

For example, in the introduction, I shared the story of my first prison break—how I learned (the hard way) that the belief that "hard work solves everything" was a con. Any good con requires a certain amount of truth to make it believable, and until my company laid me off, I could always pull together enough "proof" to keep myself safely behind bars. In reality, however, a considerable amount of critical information was left out of the equation, and the information I did have was spun in one direction by my well-meaning parents and by the whole society I grew up in.

That's why I bought into that belief—and let it decide the fate of my career for the next forty years. That's why it didn't matter to me that daily execution was hard. Work was supposed to be hard! You can see how these misinformed beliefs start to powerfully connect. I allowed myself to be the victim of my community's con.

To complicate things even more, within our communities—just as in prison—we tend to form "gangs": these are the clubs, teams, or groups of similarly minded folks we join forces with in hopes of bettering our "chances of survival." We join gangs to protect ourselves from the outside world. What we don't realize, however, is that the cost of this camaraderie and protection is "groupthink"— a limited way of seeing the world that encroaches on our freedom.

So how is your community putting you in cuffs, without you even knowing it? When you look at the various groups you belong to, how unbreakable are the shackles tying you to the people around you?

Take a moment to reflect on and answer the following questions:

- What was the impact of that one piece of advice, wisdom, or direction—given to you by your parents or others of authority with your best interests in mind—that turned out to be wrong?

- Through your education or personal experience as a young child through college, what did you learn and believe with great conviction that turned out to be completely false?

- What advice have you received over the years from your best friends and colleagues that was limited by the small bubble you collectively live in?

- Do your "gang members" have the same social, economic, racial, religious, age, or gender affiliation as you, thus limiting how you see the world?

- Here's a test: What was the last really uncomfortable thing you *chose* to do with a different gang, all by yourself?

The old saying "Garbage in, garbage out" still holds true today. If you're getting incorrect information from those who love you, imagine how you are being imprisoned by everyone else in the world—the folks who are actually *trying* to manipulate you in order to get ahead of you in the line of life. How has each one of these issues tightened the cuffs around your wrists?

How have you bought into the con that makes up the cuffs of community?

Cuffs of Circumstances

Life circumstances may also be keeping you incarcerated. This can be true in all areas of life, whether you're talking about birth circumstances, health circumstances, career circumstances, or anything else.

For example, many people's circumstances put them in jail from the day they are born. The December 24, 2014 issue of *The Atlantic* magazine published an article titled "A Different Approach to Breaking the Cycle of Poverty." The article noted that, in many areas, "a child raised in the bottom-fifth of income levels has only a 4 percent chance of rising to the top-fifth income level." You didn't ask to be born into an economically depressed inner city with terrible schools. Nevertheless, this is your lot in life—and the belief that you're stuck with it is a factor in keeping you in jail.

Gender, ethnicity, age, schooling, physical handicaps and diseases, changes in company management—all of these are examples of the cuffs of circumstances.

So what's your story? How have you been using circumstances to define who you are? Which circumstances in particular have tightened the cuffs around your wrists? Ask yourself these questions:

- How did the area where you grew up limit your view of the world?

- What impact has bad health had on your ability to do what you want to do?

- How have the difficult circumstances of others (parents, children, spouse, employers) derailed your world?

Synonyms for circumstance are "fate," "destiny," and "doom." The circumstances of your life are not necessarily your fault. Often it's the luck of the draw. But circumstances still have the ability to become cuffs in your life, powerfully constraining your ability to move forward. What circumstances in your life today are defining and controlling your destiny?

Cuffs of Complicity

The cuffs of community and circumstance are often imposed by what society was saying or doing to you. With both of these, you could make the claim, "I was just an innocent bystander who got swept up in the circumstances and the con."

Complicity is different. This is about your role in the incarceration process. What are you saying to yourself that's putting you in jail? Do you have positive, affirming self-talk going on in your head, or are you the biggest naysayer and critic of your life?

For example, when top-ranking PGA golfer Jason

Day sets himself up for a shot, he lines up behind the ball, focuses on his target down the fairway, and closes his eyes. As you watch on TV, you see his eyelids fluttering with the vision of what he's about to do. Then he opens his eyes, marches up to the ball, and proceeds to smash it three hundred-plus yards down the fairway—just as he told himself he would.

My preshot routine, meanwhile, isn't quite as solid or repeatable as Jason Day's. I stroll into the tee box yelling over to my partner Rob, "$*&@! This is the hole with the water?! I *always* hit the ball into the *&@^%$# water." Then, with one final glance at the water, I rear up and fly one straight into the water.

The cuffs of complicity really boil down to one key thing: the story that's real and true, versus the story you make up about it. As well-known author Stephen R. Covey writes in *The 7 Habits of Highly Effective People*, "You see the world not as it is but as you are—or as you are conditioned to see it." You want to be free, to do big things, and to live an extraordinary life. But the voices in your head and the stories you're making up have you in a stranglehold so tight you can't even move.

To figure out how tight a hold the cuffs of complicity have on you, use these questions:

- How much control do you feel you have over your life?

- Think about the last few challenges or unplanned circumstances you've been faced with. Did you take responsibility for your part in the situation, or were you a victim with a list of excuses?

- On a scale of 1 to 10 (low to high), how much do you believe in your ability to achieve your dreams?

Cuffs of Possessions

Our society as a whole promotes the idea of great freedom. But ironically, it also twists the idea of freedom into false hopes and promises through powerful manipulation. One of the strongest examples of this is what I call the cuffs of possessions—the constant striving for possessions, power, and position.

The engine behind our society is capitalism. According to Webster, *capitalism* is "an economic system characterized by private or corporate ownership of capital goods . . . and by prices, production, and the distribution of goods that are determined mainly by competition in a free market."

That's a mouthful, so here's a simpler definition: "If everybody does his or her job and buys stuff, then you have a job to make stuff, so you can go buy some more stuff."

This sure seems like a vicious loop in which to find yourself. It's along the lines of the hamster spinning the wheel in its cage—or should I say its prison? According to Statista, Inc., in 2016 the American advertising machine spent $200 billion on media ads alone. That number jumped to $600 billion on a worldwide basis. You yourself will personally be touched by media ads more than five thousand (and some believe as many as twenty thousand) times a day.

There's one simple goal behind this massive machine: to convince you that you must have "stuff." And behind the bright and shiny new gadget, clothes, car, house, perfume, or vacation, guess what? There's a hidden chain and shackles with your name on it. According to *Money* magazine, the average American household has more than $16,000 in credit card debt. Not only do we need it "now," but we're also willing to leverage our future to have it.

And I see you over there looking smug, thinking, "Not me." You're thrifty, and you'd never get sucked into that madness. No, you manage your money well. You go in the other door at the grocery store to avoid those little Girl Scouts and their cookies. According to your calculations, which you've double and triple checked, after only ten more years of hiding out in the bathroom when the check comes at the restaurant, you'll feel secure.

Nice try. You spend so much time thinking and worrying about money—or lack of it—that you're confined by the cuffs of possessions right along with the rest of us. The only difference between your jail cell of thrift versus that of the overspender is the color of your jailhouse walls. Incarceration is incarceration.

So how tightly do the cuffs of possessions have you in their grip? Ask yourself these questions:

- How much time do you spend thinking and/or worrying about money?

- Do you impulsively buy something you don't need for immediate satisfaction, only to be disappointed and frustrated later?

- If you wanted to make a hard left turn in your career right now that required taking a significant cut in pay, could and/or would you do it? How much are debt or other financial commitments the controlling factors in your life decisions?

- Are you currently working sixty to seventy hours a week, while putting the rest of your life on hold, for the promised panaceas of power, prestige, and position?

You live in a society that measures success by material worth—a world where you are constantly bombarded by a professional marketing machine that spends millions of dollars to enroll you in its definition of success, purpose, and significance. To escape the cuffs of possessions, you're going to need a lot of vigilance and a reshaping of how you see money.

Cuffs of Authority

The cuffs of authority are also known as "the cuffs of power and people."

In 1973, Dr. Zimbardo of the psychology department of Stanford University posed this question in the *New York Times*: "To what extent do we allow ourselves to become imprisoned by docilely accepting the roles others assign us or, indeed, choose to remain prisoners because being passive and dependent frees us from the need to act and be responsible for our actions?"

The title of Zimbardo's article was "The Mind Is a Formidable Jailer." And the answer to his question is, "More than we like to think." Worst of all, every time we meekly submit to the powers that be, we slap the cuffs of authority on ourselves.

The pros and cons of abusive authoritarian power are no great mystery. We all know there are times in a crisis where one voice, fully in charge, can be the difference between life and death. But in a more general sense, at ground level here, what's the impact on your freedom when an authoritarian ruler invades your life?

The power of authority figures in our lives is huge. These individuals have one of the most influential impacts on your freedom. That's not always a bad thing. Great leaders take off the shackles and allow you to grow. Unfortunately, the control freaks and inexperienced leaders you cross paths with during your life not only put the shackles on; they cinch them down so tight that even after the person who put them on is long gone, the cuffs themselves leave an impression that can keep you in jail forever.

Ask yourself: Where is the impact of the cuffs of authority showing up in your life?

- How have the authority figures in your life formed your attitudes toward authority?

- How are the authority figures in your life today empowering or suppressing you?

- How safe do you feel expressing an opinion to an authority figure (boss, police officer, pastor, etc.)? What drives that expression?

Sometimes, we do not get a say about the authority figures in our lives, whether they are parents, teachers, military leaders, or law enforcement officials. But often we do. Frequently, the major authority figure we're dealing with is a direct supervisor or a key client for our business. When that happens, you do have a choice as to whether you're going to remain a victim. Choose wisely.

Cuffs of Systems

Even when you take people, possessions, and circumstances out of the picture, you still have a heavy pair of shackles weighing you down: the cuffs of systems.

The systems of society constrain all of us. Now understand that, being a logical individual (who is trained as an engineer), I'm actually a fan of systems. In order to keep us from aimlessly walking around bumping into each other in society, we need guiding systems and processes. But let me qualify my statement: I'm a fan of systems that work.

Unfortunately, most systems don't work very well. And by and large, it's the dysfunctional ones that are confiscating our freedom.

Let's just jump straight to the government classic: the Department of Motor Vehicles (DMV). One of my wife's employees, Susie (who is homeless), had her belongings stolen, along with her ID. My wife took her to the DMV to replace the ID so that Susie could perform simple life tasks, such as getting a phone.

After gathering all the things required per the DMV website's instructions, standing in two lines (one of which was a screening line to ensure that you had everything you needed), and waiting ninety minutes, Susie finally made it to a window to see a clerk—where she was told that she was missing a document that hadn't been on the Internet checklist.

"There's a new law," the clerk told her.

"What, in the last five minutes?" Susie demanded, understandably angry. But there was nothing she could do. A security person was circling behind her. She could walk out or be escorted out, and that was that. Come back when you've learned to follow the rules!

So you thought you were free? Think again. The system has you. And the bigger and more complex the system, the more likely the chance of dysfunction. And don't even get me started on health insurance, our tax codes, airlines, or any of the other arbitrary and bureaucratic obstacles we face every day here in "the land of the free."

As a leader and as a person, how are you more shackled by society's systems than you need to be?

- What systems are you forced to use that are causing you frustration?

- What system in your life is controlling you, versus you controlling it?

- When and where are you using technology or systems to hide from the world?

- What systems have you implemented in your business that are strangling your team?

Unless living in a tent in the mountains is an option, you will need to be able to negotiate the multitiered systems of society if you plan on breaking out of jail.

Assess Your Prison

How free are you? Are you the warden? Or are you a prisoner tightly cuffed by the shackles of the society we live in—a prison with guards at every corner to keep you in line and following the herd, so that you'll keep your head down and continue playing small? Just how much mobility do you really have?

> How incarcerated are you?
> Take our free online assessment at
> www.jailbreakleadership.com

I have an image from high school that has never left my mind. The town I lived in had just built this amazing new high school, complete with its own field house and sprawling multiwinged campus. With the excess capacity, one of the wings was dedicated to a group of grade school kids.

I was heading into the cafeteria for lunch one day when I observed how the grade school teachers kept their charges on a very short leash. The kids were all standing single file, and the teachers were ordering them to stay in line and stop talking—all while directing the kids to their next destination.

The difference in freedom and control between these grade school kids and me, as a junior in high school, struck me. Every action they took seemed to be controlled by the teachers in charge, while I had the freedom to sit, eat, and talk to anyone I wanted.

The fact that I was responding to a ringing bell that told me exactly where to be for the next thirty-five minutes, until the next bell sounded, was lost on me. I could see only the elementary kids' lack of choice, while I assumed that I had great personal freedom.

Now that you've had a crash course in the shackles of society, how has your assessment of your personal freedom changed? Are you the high school student, watching the people in your world and seeing their incarceration while completely missing your own? Or have you noticed how much you are still responding to the bells that tell you where to be and when?

When you start to identify the various "cuffs" keeping

you in prison, you begin to reclaim control of your life—both as a person and as a leader. This is the power of questioning what's true, versus what's a manipulation or half-truth.

You are the judge and jury of your life. And now that you know what's going on, you get to give your own verdict. If you'd like to change your level of incarceration, embrace who you really are, and have the freedom to lead a life—and an organization—of success and significance, read on. There's a custom escape plan waiting for you.

Chapter 3

The Key

"Only humans have to struggle to discover their proper role in the whole scheme of things. We are the only ones who seek meaning, purpose, and happiness."

—*Girolamo Savonarola*

The Great Escape

The movie *The Great Escape*—released in 1963 and starring Steve McQueen and James Garner—is based on a true story from World War II.

Here's what happened. Because they were spending enormous resources dealing with Allied escapees, the Germans decided to put all the prisoners bent on escaping in one place—the better to keep an eye on all those rascals.

Thus, a German task force rounded up the trouble-makers and relocated them to an exclusive high-security prison—Stalag Luft III—specifically built to contain them. There, the POWs were put under the watchful eye of Colonel Oberst von Luger of the Luftwaffe.

In retrospect, this may not have been the Germans' best idea.

Putting together hundreds of prisoners with the same focused purpose led to a massive escape plan—which then led to seventy-six prisoners breaking loose into the German countryside.

As much as those POWs undoubtedly wanted out of the Nazi prison camp, the Allied soldiers who escaped that day didn't do it just for themselves. They had a larger purpose: to create a huge disruption to Germany's war effort. The prisoners believed that if the Germans were distracted by chasing the Allied escapees, they wouldn't be able to kill as many other Allied soldiers.

That driving purpose became the key to one of the greatest jailbreaks in history. And it can break you out of jail too.

The 3P Key

The fastest, easiest way to open any jail cell is with a key. In our case—breaking free of the shackles of society rather than a Nazi prison camp—that key has a name.

I call it the "3P Key."

3P KEY

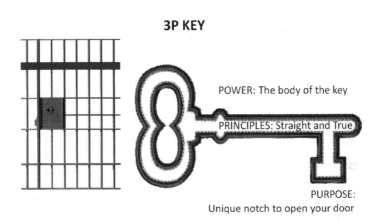

POWER: The body of the key

PRINCIPLES: Straight and True

PURPOSE:
Unique notch to open your door

Figure 3.1

The 3P Key is unique to you. You forge it yourself from three things that make up the core of who you are: your power, your principles, and your purpose.

Your 3P Key represents the perfect you—the version that the master designer had in mind before you ever got here. Forging your 3P Key is about discovering and aligning three things: your natural strengths and talents, the values you deem most important in your life, and what you have been called to do in this world. When these three things line up, you have the perfect key to break you out of your particular prison. And trust me on this: to successfully escape from the constraints of your jail, you will have to be the best you can be!

As an example, in our society we are drawn to the greats in sports. LeBron James, the "King" of the NBA as of 2017, is a great exemplar of embracing and fine-tuning the 3P Key. He has obviously been blessed with the physical attributes for being a basketball player—his natural strengths. But the NBA has quite a few 6' 8" 250-pound ballplayers in the league.

So what makes James exceptional?

It's not just his attributes, but the continuous evolution of his skills from season to season—and where he chooses to apply them—that sets him apart. It's the way he lives his values, like taking a big pay cut (and all the heat from the press) to go to Miami in search of the holy grail—the NBA championship—or returning to his home city of Cleveland to end its fifty-year title drought. And finally, it is the way he uses his success to create significance. On the LeBron James Family website—his nonprofit for kids—James says, "Our strength is our legacy." He is an example of power, principles, and purpose in action.

Few of us are called to be or have been given the exact same gifts as a LeBron James. But can you say that you have fully embraced who you are, like James has? As a business leader, is what you do all about the bottom line, scoring points, and getting more? Or do you lead an organization built on significance—an organization about your employees, their families, your customers, and your vendors?

Your strength is your legacy. Discovering, embracing, developing, and delivering on your 3P Key is the only way to open the door to the kind of world you will leave behind.

LeBron James and the prisoners in *The Great Escape* have something in common: they provide a blueprint for anyone looking to construct the key to opening his or her jailhouse door. This chapter will walk you through the process of building your personal 3P Key, by helping you identify your individual power, principles, and purpose.

Power

The first P in the 3P Key—power—represents the key blank.

Your power represents the collective strengths and talents you possess (and can put to use in your escape from jail). This is the foundation that your key will be constructed from.

When we talk about power, we are talking about questions like these: What's available to help facilitate your escape? When all else is taken from you, what strengths and talents do you have, and how can you creatively use them to support your planned escape?

If you're thinking, "I don't have any special powers," I have some great news for you. Just like everyone else in the world, you came standard from the factory with a core set of talents.

You may not know exactly what they are yet, but on some level you've been leaning into these gifts all your life. There are tasks in your life that are easy, and other tasks that require a full-on struggle to complete. The things that are easy to do are your strengths. Those natural talents, once identified and developed, represent your most powerful ally in mobilizing your escape from jail.

Just as prisoners fashion escape tools from seemingly innocent objects, your power allows you to creatively take what's available, modify it, and use it in new and powerful ways to achieve your purpose. If you're going to have any chance of breaking out of your jail, you need to recognize the gifts you have and develop them into powerful tools to reach the freedom you desire.

In other words, in order to escape, you need to be the best you can be. And working to your power will always give you the best advantage possible.

So how do you figure out what your power is?

You figure it out by assessing what you've got—and then connecting the dots.

Assess Your Power

When it comes to spotting our own power, a lot of us have trouble seeing the forest for all the trees. Luckily for us, we have a handy tool at our disposal: self-assessment tests.

Self-assessment tests are an incredible way to help you self-profile your strengths. Knowing why and how you work best is an invaluable asset in your pursuit of freedom, and these tests give you that knowledge. With mind-numbing accuracy, you can explore everything about yourself: talents, work methods, spiritual gifts, personality types, leadership styles, temperament, motivations—and the list goes on.

I myself am a self-assessment test junkie, and I've probably taken every one of them under the sun— Myers-Briggs, DiSC, 360 Degree Feedback, Kolbe, you name it. My all-time favorite, though, is a test called StrengthsFinder.

StrengthsFinder is based on Gallup poll data that has identified thirty-four core talents. The test identifies your top five talents. While we all have some level of talent in the other twenty-nine areas, these five represent your natural talents, or your personal strengths. When you're engaged in activities connected to your strengths, you notice that you have a natural ability for them: the tasks are easy to perform as well as fun to do.

For example, one of my StrengthsFinder talents is

called "strategic." People with this strength can quickly spot the relevant patterns and issues and create alternative ways to proceed.

I use this strength constantly when I work with groups of people who are trying to solve complex, difficult problems. Quite honestly, a lot of the time, I have the least expertise of anyone in the room when it comes to the problem we're talking about. After about ten minutes of endless talk with no direction in sight, however, I can go to a whiteboard, draw a picture, restate what I heard in a few short sentences, and ask, "Is this what we're talking about?"

Like magic, the logjam breaks. The group takes a direction, and we are off and running. I don't know how I do this. I just do it. In fact, I could do it all day long and never break a sweat. That is my strategic strength in action. It's kind of fun and surprisingly easy.

Who doesn't like doing things that are easy and fun?

The first step in breaking out of jail is to get clear about what's already in your hand. Taking the StrengthsFinder assessment at www.gallupstrengthscenter.com is a must. It will give you a powerful head start in figuring out your talents. Until then, try asking yourself these questions:

- What tasks in life do you find easy to do?

- What things do people always come to you for?

- What do you do that gives you energy, instead of draining you?

You cannot have enough self-awareness. Understanding your strengths will give you confidence and show you the skills and creativity you have at your disposal as you discover your unique path to freedom. And that's only the beginning.

Connect the Dots

I know what you're thinking. "Okay, Jeff, self-assessment tests are great and everything, but where's the deliverable here? How does this stuff connect to my real life?"

To find the answer to that question, you have to connect the dots.

Connecting the dots starts with identifying an area of your life where you've consistently enjoyed doing the work, found it relatively easy to do, and ultimately found success.

One of the best places to look for things like this is your hobbies. I haven't met anyone with a serious hobby who didn't find it easy and fun, and who hadn't reached some level of mastery in that area. Let's face it: why would you do something in your spare time that you didn't find highly fulfilling?

Perform this same exercise regarding your job. Even if you're not a big fan of your current position, in most cases there are aspects of it you do enjoy. As with your hobbies, go through the process of identifying what you like to do.

After you've identified the things you do that work for you, step back and analyze what's occurring when you're involved in those activities. Simply ask yourself, "What is it about this hobby or task that I enjoy most? What elements or activities within it do I naturally take to?"

Record your answers on a piece of paper—and then connect the dots between what you enjoy and the personal strengths you identified in the StrengthsFinder test. Which talents are you using when you're performing the activities you listed? Can you spot where one, two, or more strengths are coming into play?

Once you see how your strengths play out in your real life, you can start to apply more of the actions that work for you to your role as leader in your organization. And that's when you really "get jacked."

Get Jacked

As great as each of your individual strengths is, your true power zone comes from combining strengths and applying them in the world. Engaging in two or more of your strengths at once has a kind of multiplier effect that sets you apart from the rest of the crowd. How do you synergize all this power?

You do it by combining your talents with your skills and experience.

I call this "getting jacked." In the prison environment,

getting jacked is all about becoming the biggest and baddest dude in the yard. Picture a prison yard full of monstrous men, pumping everything but the prison walls in an attempt to pack on more muscle. Do you want to mess with those guys?

Probably not. And when you get jacked, nothing and no one is going to mess with you, either.

Finding the intersection where your talents meet your skills and experience gives you the chance to really up your game. This is what will give you the most power possible to take on the biggest fight of your life—the fight for the freedom to live and lead outside the prison walls created by our status-driven, fear-ridden society.

Each time you lean in to your talents, you have the opportunity to draw on and enhance your experience (the facts and lessons you've learned from life so far) and your skills (inherent strengths). This should become a continuous loop of building, growing, and developing yourself, both as a person and as a leader. In the yard, prisoners get stronger by dedicating their time to beefing themselves up. Your challenge is to place yourself in situations where you can continue to expand your power.

To get jacked, ask yourself the following questions:

- What talents do you naturally integrate and use together?

- Which activities best showcase your combination of strengths, talents, and experiences?

- What steps can you take to further embrace the capabilities you possess?

Power Tools

The most common weapon known to convicts is called the "shiv." A shiv is a weapon crudely constructed from what's available: spoons, shoelaces, bed slats, combs, tape, typewriter carriages, or toothbrushes, to name a few. Shivs are made by taking everyday innocent items available in the closed environment of a prison and transforming them into weapons for survival.

You now have a list of natural talents at your disposal. Do they remain interesting concepts, or are you ready to transform your talents into powerful tools?

If the answer to that last question is the latter, that's a sign you're ready to step into your power. And when you tap into that force, you bring the possibility of escape from prison within reach.

Principles

Just having natural power alone isn't enough. You need to be able to direct that power in a way that best helps you reach your goal of becoming a Jailbreak Leader. For that, we have the second piece of the 3P Key: principles.

Your principles are your values—the things you feel are important to you, and the yardsticks you use to define success. They ensure you're delivering on who you want to be in the world. Even better, your principles are what keep you on track as you move forward with your great escape.

You can think about this as driving down a country road late at night. You have no moon, no stars—just pitch black. And instead of a line dividing the road, all you see is black asphalt disappearing into the horizon.

But lining both sides of the road at short intervals are little posts, each topped with a white reflector. Those reflectors bounce the light from your headlights back at you. Outside the boundary of the posts on either side is nothing but danger, a dark abyss of rocks and trees that would surely bring your journey to a screeching halt. But in spite of the world beyond your vision, you know this: the more you stay to the center of the road between the posts, the safer you are and the faster you can travel toward your destination.

Those guideposts are your principles.

Most Jailbreak Leaders have anywhere from five to eight principles to maximize their power and keep them on track toward their goals. How do you define yours?

Try this expanded version of an exercise first defined

by Stephen Covey in *The 7 Habits of Highly Effective People.*

> In your mind's eye, picture yourself attending a funeral. As you walk inside the building, you notice the flowers, the soft organ music. You see the faces of friends and family you pass along the way. You feel the shared sorrow of losing, and the joy of having known, which radiates from the hearts of the people there.

> As you walk down to the front of the room and look inside the casket, you suddenly come face to face with yourself. This is your funeral, three years from today. All these people have come to honor you, to express feelings of love and appreciation for your life.

> As you take a seat and wait for the services to begin, you look at the program in your hand. There'll be three speakers. The first speaker represents your family, both immediate and extended: partner, children, brothers, sisters, nephews, nieces, mother, and father. Also represented are friends from your high school, local social club, college, and neighborhood, who have come from all over the country.

The second speaker is from your work or your profession.

The third is from a community organization where you've been involved in service, such as a church.

Now think deeply. What would you like each of these speakers to say about you and your life? What kind of husband, wife, father, or mother would you like their words to reflect? What kind of son or daughter? What kind of work associate?

What character would you like them to have seen in you? What contributions, what achievements would you want them to remember? Look carefully at the people around you. What difference would you like to have made in their lives?

Take a few minutes to write out the three speeches from your funeral. This is both your definition of success and the significance you have created in the lives of others. This is what you want to be able to give, how you want your work and relationships to be. This is you, successfully being your best you.

When you complete the speeches, go back and read through them. Wouldn't that day be a great moment of celebration, knowing you delivered significance to the people in your life?

Now take your picture of success and build the guide-posts for your journey—the foundational stakes in the ground that will help ensure you successfully make it down that road. Make a list of the words in your speeches that identify your core values. You may see some words repeated often. When this happens, take note, because it means that this particular value has special meaning to you.

You may see some words in the speeches that have similar meaning. In those cases, which word is most powerful? Or is there still another word that better describes your desire?

Next, pare down your list. Simplicity is important. What are your core words? Think of the words you truly need to guide your path, just as the guideposts did along that dark country road. Again, you may have as few as five and as many as eight. It's your list; you decide what you need.

Finally, once you have your list, the last step in this process is to add your definition to each word. What does this word mean to you? Your definition should be measurable and simple, using only three to five words. It's critical to know how well you're exhibiting your principles. Either you're on the path or you're not. Either you're in the center of the road holding your values tight, or you're on the fringes, about to go off the course.

Here are a few examples of clearly defined principles:

- **Passion:** Positive "can-do" attitude
- **Empathy**: Constant awareness of feelings
- **Fun:** Enjoying the process

What's your list?

Defining your principles calls on you to clarify what you already know to be important and to motivate yourself to do the work that matters most to you. It empowers you with a sense of boldness for what you are doing. Once you have strong principles riding shotgun, they form the second part of your 3P Key—accelerating your journey toward your escape from jail and the end vision for your life.

Purpose

One of the biggest questions everyone in the human race is called to answer is, "What am I supposed to be doing with my life?"

When it comes to breaking out of jail, the answer to this question is the third and final piece of your 3P Key: your purpose.

While power and principles define what you are and how you do what you do, purpose determines what you do with what you have. The power of a clear and well-defined purpose is unmistakable. Understanding your purpose is a game changer. It releases you from the shackles of society and frees you to pursue life with an entirely new level of fearlessness and tenacity. It becomes the banks of the river that is you, bringing clarity and focus to who you are and where you can be your best self.

And here's some more good news: just as you came prepackaged with strengths and talents, you also came wired with your personal purpose.

Your job is to discover what your inbuilt purpose is. And you can do that through something that I like to call "unscripted moments."

Unscripted Moments

What are "unscripted moments"?

Unscripted moments are random moments in time when you automatically respond to an outside, unplanned stimulus, using your personal strengths in a powerful and natural way for the benefit of others.

You've been participating in unscripted moments all your life. But because these moments last for only a few seconds and come as naturally as breathing to you, their significance often goes unnoticed. Nevertheless, these moments in time are where your purpose has been hiding, waiting to be revealed.

You can distinguish unscripted moments from other moments in your life in three ways:

1. **They are caused by a unique external stimulus that catapults you into action.** Often, this stimulus is deep-rooted frustration with something that you see occurring, or some injustice you see in the world that you strongly believe is "just not right."

2. **They spark an immediate action or response in you.** There's no thinking involved in an unscripted moment. You see it, and you immediately bolt out of your seat into action. You automatically know what to do. During an unscripted moment, your reaction bypasses your "lizard brain," making you fearless for a brief moment in time. You can't help yourself, and you innately know what to do. It's kind of like magic.

3. **The outcome benefits others.** Unscripted moments are always for the benefit of someone else. And more often than not, you end up with a positive response to your actions. The outcome usually resolves the deep-rooted frustration or injustice that caused you to act in the first place.

It is very important to note that only the first few seconds of an event—from the stimulus to your initial action—are important in discovering your unscripted moments. As the rest of the event evolves, all your filters start to kick in, other people get involved, and the outcome will be what it will be. For our discovery purposes, your focus should be on what caused you to jump into action.

It's important to note that unscripted moments most often won't be life-threatening or lifesaving events. If you kept your kid from stepping off the curb and getting hit by a bus, that doesn't qualify as an unscripted moment. That's called being a parent. Unscripted moments are also not just anything that causes you to get angry, such as someone cutting you off while you're driving. That's called road rage. Unscripted moments are always rooted in a positive response to a wrong or need.

One of my favorite examples of an unscripted moment in action comes from a guy I know named Steve. I met Steve several years ago on a ranch in Montana during a three-month sabbatical. Steve and I were among a group of ten men—all strangers to me—looking for a little time to regroup and focus on silence and solitude.

After observing him for a couple of days, I noticed one thing about Steve that I wasn't quite sure was real. At mealtime, as soon as we finished eating, Steve would always jump up to clear everyone's plates. If something needed to be done in the kitchen, Steve was there. If we went on a hike, we had to physically fight off Steve's attempts to carry our knapsacks for us. One day, we spotted a forest fire a few miles away, and it was Steve's unstoppable impulse to help put it out that mobilized the rest of us to do exactly that—a bonding experience we'll never forget.

I've never met anybody more about service than Steve. Service is at the heart of all his unscripted moments. And that's why being of service is at the core of his purpose.

To discover the purpose buried in your unscripted moments, walk yourself through the following exercise.

Unscripted Moments

Think about something that consistently frustrates you—a particular person, event, or situation. Home in on your unscripted reaction to that "something."

Now write out the story of one of your unscripted moments in great detail:

- Describe the situation where you just jumped into action to resolve an issue.

- Did the event involve anything specific about age, gender, social class, or environment?

- What did other people do or, more likely, not do in the immediate moment?

Describe your actions again in great detail:

- What was the very first thing you did?

- Was there a plan, or did you just act?

- When you look at your actions, how do they line up with your power?

Next, describe the stimulus in great detail:

- Describe the frustration or injustice that was happening.

- What's the one word to describe the emotion you were feeling?

- Is there something in your history that made this event real or emotional for you?

Describe the initial outcome:

- What do you have to say about what happened?

- What did other people say about what happened?

- What was the result?

After spending time on this story, what other similar stories come to mind?

- What are the common themes?
- Was the stimulus the same, or a version of something similar?
- Are your actions similar across all the events?

Once you understand your unscripted moments, you can develop your personal purpose statement.

Your Personal Purpose Statement

As great as your purpose may be, it's not going to do you or anyone else any good unless you act on it. For that reason, your personal purpose statement will consist of two things: action and outcome.

Your action is what you do in response to the stimulus in your unscripted moment. It's your power and principles (strengths, natural talents, skills, and experience) in action.

Your outcome is the positive result you desire from your actions, relative to the frustration or injustice you identified in your unscripted moment.

The combination of action and outcome forms your two-word purpose statement.

For example, in Steve's case, the action he couldn't keep from doing in his unscripted moments was offering help to others. Seeing a need always threw him into action. The outcome he hoped to achieve from offering that help was to take care of the rest of us.

Steve's personal purpose statement is this:

Offering Care

Here are a few more purpose statements, along with what their owners do professionally in the world.

Releasing Authenticity: The ability to allow others to express the truth about themselves

Professionally: A video producer bringing personal stories alive

Bridging Truth: Connecting people of diversity to know and understand the truth about each other

Professionally: Founder and president of a social enterprise putting the homeless to work in the community and educating the housed and unhoused on commonalities and challenges

Engaging Beauty: Finding what's beautiful in what's normally perceived as ugly

Professionally: Executive director of a community development organization and founder and president of a hair salon

Equipping Success: Hands-on problem solver especially focused on individuals without resources

Professionally: Founder and owner of a mortgage company with a unique service model of supporting challenging projects

Exhorting Potential: Ability to see what is possible while holding individuals and groups to a higher standard

Professionally: Pastor of a large church

Here is an example of purpose in action. Over lunch with the video producer I mentioned in the first example on this list—"releasing authenticity"—I asked him, "How is your purpose showing up for you?"

He had just returned from his biggest project to date, a commercial shoot in Los Angeles. The day of the shoot, he'd had twenty people on site, plus the customer had flown in to watch. "I was feeling pretty anxious and stressed out," he told me, explaining how he'd been trying to control both the action and the outcome. But then he stepped back for a moment and thought, *What is really the best thing I can do right now?*

Instantly, his simple purpose statement appeared front and center: "releasing authenticity." He said, "I immediately decided to reach out to each of the people there, including the customer, to have a brief conversation." In those conversations, he used his natural power to release the authenticity of each person and to allow them to do what they did best. In the process, he delegated a couple of managerial tasks that had been holding things back, and they were off to the races.

"Jeff, we had the most amazing result ever," he told me. "Everyone stepped up with unbelievable creativity, we had a fun experience, and the outcome was greater than I could have imagined."

My own personal purpose statement is "mobilizing possibilities." In my unscripted moments, my frustration shows up when individuals or groups come up with a thousand reasons why they're stuck in a certain situation. That just drives me nuts. What's wrong with these people? Why can't they see what could be? The outcome—or what I bring to the party—is to help the group become fully engaged in identifying all the "possibilities" and "mobilizing" them into action.

"Mobilizing possibilities." Why do you think I wrote this book? I want you to see the possibilities in your life, to look beyond the constraints of your jail and to go for it! That's my purpose.

What's yours?

When you reflect on your unscripted moments, how would you describe what you're doing? How would someone observing you describe your actions? Because you are probably using some combination of your strengths, what one action word would describe what you are doing when you are using all your strengths and talents?

Then, what is the outcome you are trying to achieve? This is often the opposite of the frustration or injustice you see in the world. For example, when I mobilize possibilities, I want to create a world without restrictions. You can also look to your principles to discover the outcome you're searching for, because very strong principles can be clues to what you want to see more of in the world.

Feel free to get out the thesaurus and play with these concepts until you come up with a purpose statement that resonates with you and that captures what you do perfectly, in just two words.

Your personal purpose is the final piece in the 3P Key to unlocking your jail. It opens the door of possibility and offers you the freedom to live and lead as your most authentic self. It's the *one* critical thing we're all depending on you, as a leader, to give us. It's what you do.

When you own your purpose, you become a magnet for opportunities, and you learn to deliver on that purpose with more intention, power, and authority than you have ever had in the past. And that's when you can really start to flex your muscles as a Jailbreak Leader.

Potential: Unlocked

Take a page from *The Great Escape*. If the 3P Key process can successfully facilitate the largest mass escape of WWII POWs from a specially built prison in a wartime environment, it can most certainly provide you with your best chance of escaping all the constraints you're facing in your personal prison.

When you're living and leading with your 3Ps, you're being the best person you can be, no matter where you are or what you're doing. You're leaning into what you were ultimately designed to do. And that can create tremendous results.

The 3P Key opens the door to your jailhouse. Now that you're armed with the understanding of your best you, clarity about what you do, and guideposts to keep the end in mind, it is time to open the door. In the next chapter, you'll see what the world has to offer outside the prison cell of your mind—and how to overcome the wall of fear to reach the freedom that's waiting on the other side.

Chapter 4

The Call

There is no greater gift you can give or receive than to honor your calling. It's why you were born. And how you become most truly alive.

—*Oprah Winfrey*

Sound the Alarm

With your 3P Key finally in hand, you step forward and insert it into your jailhouse door. The key turns with considerable effort, until you hear the clanking thud of the lock releasing the door.

You grab the bars of the door, and with all your might, you give it a huge push.

Your jailhouse door swings wide open. Instantly, a blast of light and fresh air hits you. Before your eyes lies the most beautiful sight you have ever seen: freedom.

But even as the view takes your breath away, the reality of your situation hits you, dropping on your head like a sack of bricks. *You are still in jail.* The minute you step across that threshold, every alarm in your prison is going to go off.

In fact, you don't even need to take a step first. They're already at it.

"What do you think you are doing?" the first alarm screams. "Being in jail has it problems, but at least you know what to expect!" screeches another, wailing over your lack of competency. "I don't care how self-aware you think you are with your new purpose, power, and principles," they all shriek together. "You will not last ten minutes on the other side!"

And the sad part is, it's true.

According to an article in the June 2015 issue of *The Atlantic*, "More than 92 percent of fugitives from medium- and high-security prisons were captured within a year, and that estimate is conservative."

"They spend a lot of energy trying to figure out how to escape," said Patricia Hardyman, associate director of the Association of State Correctional Administrators, in that same article. "But then they don't make very good plans about what to do once they get out."

The reality of staging a successful prison break is that you have to be prepared to fight for your freedom on both sides of the wall. It is time to figure out what, exactly, you are going to do with this freedom you aspire to. And for that, you need more than a key to the outside.

You need a calling.

The Call

You now have the key to unlock the jail you've been trapped in all your life. But even with the door to your prison cell swinging open in front of you, escape isn't going to be easy. You're not going to stroll out of this maximum-security compound whistling and waving a cheerful farewell to all the armed guards posted in the watchtowers.

No, you have a fight ahead of you. One that could very well take every ounce of energy you have, if you want to win it. To persevere to the end of this escape attempt—and to stay free once you break loose—you're going to need one heck of a strong reason to push through all the resistance that awaits you on the way to your goal.

That reason to push through is what I like to dub "the call to freedom."

Your call is your most fundamental why—the sweet spot and ultimate use of your purpose. It is that place in life where you create not just success for yourself, but greater significance. It is the way you give back to the world.

Your call goes beyond you. It is your reason for giving your purpose away.

A great way to think about your call is to imagine an archery target. You know, the round target set downfield with a set of colored circles on it—and that red bull's-eye smack in the middle. The target represents your purpose. If you, as the archer, shoot and miss the target altogether, that's like working outside your purpose. Any time you hit the target, you are on purpose. And when you hit your sweet spot—the bull's-eye in the middle—that is your call.

When you embrace your call, it becomes the unstoppable catalyst you need in order to take action. Your call is the life source of the powerful "why" you will keep with you throughout your great escape from jail. It is the compelling reason you will be willing to go against what you have been told, what society promises, and the alarms of fear, in order to achieve your ends.

Here is the reality of life. If you want to venture toward freedom, success, and significance, you are going to be going up against everything and everybody. If you are going to take that risk, you'd better have a really good reason and, unlike our many failed fugitives, a solid path to follow.

So if you are in, and your gut tells you that it's going to be worth it, let's go figure this out. This chapter will help you discover your personal call and show you how to build a vision for your future that directly revolves around your calling.

Discover Your Call

Just as we were all born with unique power and purpose, we all have a unique call that innately belongs to us. So where is yours hiding?

In the same way that you have been randomly using your power—and randomly expressing your purpose via unscripted moments—you have also had experiences where you engaged with the sweet spot of your call. And just as your power, principles, and passion were already there, waiting for you to recognize them, the gift of your call just needs to be unwrapped, as well, so you can see what's inside.

As a starting point, once you have received the gift of your 3P Key, finding the first clue to your calling is a matter of looking deeper inside that package to see the components of the call:

1. Where in life are you already fulfilling your purpose? Identify those times where all aspects of your power, principles, and purpose naturally come into play.

2. Where within the use of your purpose are you experiencing the most passion? What is that aspect of your purpose that most energizes and excites you—and causes you to feel a compelling need to do the work?

3. Finally, within those first two parameters, which sliver of your purpose gives you the greatest satisfaction *where the result is not about you*, but is for the benefit of others? Remember, success is about you, but significance is the value you bring to the larger world. This is your ultimate contribution.

Once you've narrowed it down, you're ready to put a name to the bull's-eye of your target. Ask yourself these questions:

- At the core of the activity captured by your two-word purpose, when you are at your absolute best and engaged in the activity you identified in the last exercise, **what are you doing** (action)?

- **Who** is the ideal **person** receiving your gift?

- **What** do **they** ultimately **receive** from you? What do you ultimately hope to give?

When you act on your purpose and, in the process, achieve the most rewarding outcome for others that you can imagine, you are living your call.

> **CALL**
> **(Your action)(To whom)(Outcome)**

You could pursue any number of possibilities with your purpose. However, your call creates the greatest fulfillment. It lights you up like a flashing neon sign, making you almost giddy with excitement. This is the path you are meant to pursue.

For example, I am aligned with my purpose any time I am helping others—from individuals to organizations—to "mobilize possibilities." They have opportunities, and I help to get them unstuck and moving again. That is hitting my target. For most of my professional career, this has shown up for me in executing strategic initiatives for various businesses.

My call, however, is "Free seekers to live their call." This is the ultimate use of my purpose, because the most significant possibility I could ever mobilize is freeing an individual to go after who he or she is meant to be. I found my call at the core of my larger purpose, while I was executing initiatives. It appeared at those times when everyone involved in a project felt aligned and plugged in to his or her greatest opportunities, all because of what I was doing with my 3P Key. Achieving a business objective is nice, but freeing someone to be who he or she is called to be is the greatest gift I could ever give anyone. I cannot imagine a more fulfilling and exciting way to manifest my personal purpose.

You can certainly obtain great personal success by embracing and using your purpose, without ever creating significance. Nevertheless, the currency of freedom is significance.

You can successfully apply your purpose in many ways, but there is one thing you came prewired to deliver that satisfies both success and significance. When you find it, life becomes an exciting adventure of continuous unscripted moments. You've made the transformation from just seeing and planning to actually living your call: doing what you do best where and when it is needed most.

Once you arrive at this point, the way you live—and the way you lead—will never be the same.

Dream Up Your Vision

Now that you've identified your call, you can begin to bring it into your life on purpose instead of just stumbling across it by luck. For that, you need vision.

Vision gives you context for your calling. If your purpose is what you do, and your call is the most significant expression of what you do, your vision establishes—at the highest level—where you do it, whom you are doing it for, and what you hope to accomplish in the world through it. It creates a compelling and motivating picture of what you hope for in the future. It takes the driving force of your call and makes it concrete, so that you can actually use your call as a compass to set your course and motivate you to overcome the challenges and problems you face on the journey to becoming a Jailbreak Leader.

As a business leader, you are very comfortable with the idea of creating a vision for your business. Creating this new vision is a similar exercise, but with a specific focus on integrating your call into your larger vision. You need to create a vision not only for your business, but also for all aspects of your life. We reach higher goals when all the fundamental systems in our lives are running smoothly. In this case, your "fundamental systems" are your intentions—or visions—for the four core areas of your life: work, relationships, spirituality, and health.

Your "work" includes things like your career, philanthropy (volunteering), and even your hobbies. "Relationships" simply refers to the people you interface with in your life—everyone from your friends and family, to your work associates, to the clerk at the grocery store. "Spirituality," or faith, is your personal relationship with what you believe about the realm beyond us and how it interfaces with your skills, strengths, purpose, and calling. And finally, "health" is all about looking at your body as the vehicle for delivering your vision to the world.

For additional help in defining and developing your call for each of these areas, visit www.jailbreakleadership.com.

To mobilize your vision in these four categories, write a vision statement for each core area of your life. For each one, ask yourself the following questions:

- How would you describe the desired outcome or impact you want to create by applying your purpose and calling in each of the four core categories?

- In each area of your life, who is the best recipient of your purpose and calling?

- What actions will you take to best manifest your purpose and calling in each area?

- What would your vision be for each area if you were to take your optimal idea of it today and multiply it ten times?

Begin each category with your purpose and calling. Then add vision and "painting" concepts to each area.

For example, as of this writing, here is my vision for the "work" category of my life.

PURPOSE: *To Mobilize Possibilities*

CALLING: Free seekers to live their calling.

WORK VISION: Guide five million **transformative leaders** to be **purpose driven.**

- Guide: We provide change-management expertise in combination with the process of coaching and walking the journey with the person (think "river-raft guide").

- Transformative leaders: We work with leaders who are ready to lead change and who are looking for new and creative ways to do it.

- Purpose driven: We align the personal purposes of the leader and staff so that they become a driver of the overall mission of the company.

- Blanton Group (BG) employees: Create a community where all employees know and have the opportunity to live out their purposes at work.

- BG customers: Support business leaders in their quest to lead fully integrated, purpose-driven organizations of significance.

- BG core vendors: Be a beacon for all organizations we interface with, enabling them to experience and share the power of purpose.

THE PAINTING: We provide leaders and their organizations the freedom to seize possibilities bigger than themselves through knowledge and support. We empower them to know and confidently use their power, principles, and purpose as the guiding light for creating and delivering on a powerful vision. We act as a catalyst for businesses to go beyond the bottom line to create significance and impact, based on the collective purpose and passion of the organization.

And here is what this same exercise looks like for me in the relationship category.

> **PURPOSE:** *To Mobilize Possibilities*
>
> **CALLING:** Free seekers to live their calling.
>
> **RELATIONSHIPS VISION:** Positive support for what is possible
>
> - Stay in my lane of abilities.
> - Always bring my best (3P Key) in support of others' possibilities.
> - Meet people where they are at in life.
>
> **THE PAINTING:** I bring energy, ideas, excitement, options, and action to people's ideas. When invited, I bring the best I have to offer to help them fulfill their purposes in life. I act as the positive can-do person versus the jailhouse risk-and-problem person.

Now it's your turn. Take off the brakes! Forget your current circumstances, limitations, and challenges. Embrace the view of the world from your youth, before the shackles of society stole your dreams away, and then rebuild your vision—on every level—from there. Then act on it.

Your incarceration started when you were a small kid, and it's still happening today. Understanding your purpose and calling is the foundation that anchors you in the world. But moving from incarceration to the freedom of calling is a process. While your purpose will remain steadfast, your vision will evolve as you evolve. As you shed more and more of your jailhouse thinking and become stronger in who you are, more clarity and focus will naturally come your way.

In other words, today's vision is just a starting point. But simply starting where you are today, using what is available to you, is a powerful step forward in the process of transformation.

When you create, follow, and regularly update a vision that answers the question "What does the world look like when I powerfully apply my purpose and calling?" and charges your imagination, you become a well-oiled machine of possibility, not only for your organization, but in all aspects of your life. From there, busting out of jail is just a hop and a skip away.

Step Out of Jail

Rick Warren, best-selling author of *The Purpose Driven Life*, once said in a speech, "Knowing your purpose is like graduating from kindergarten. Knowing your call is like getting a PhD."

It is sad to realize that less than a quarter of our population even think they know their purpose. And more often than not, in my experience, even among that crowd, the purposes they talk about are just fancy jailhouse talk of success.

If you have done the work to find your purpose, congratulations! That puts you in the top 20 percent of the population. If you know your call, you just became a 1 percenter. That's really something to celebrate.

But knowledge without action doesn't mean anything. You now know what mountains are available for you to conquer in your life, both personally and professionally. But there are always many roads to the top, and finding the best one for you and those who follow you can be a formidable challenge. In the next chapter, we'll bust you out of prison and send you running up the mountain with a full-fledged jailbreak.

Chapter 5

Jailbreak

Vision without action is merely a dream. Action without vision just passes the time. Vision with action changes the world.

—*Joel A. Barker*

Underestimated

The morning of January 22, 2016, kicked off a really bad day for the Orange County, California, Sheriff's Department.

The sheriffs are in charge of the Orange County Men's Jail. That day, during the 5:00 a.m. body count, they discovered three inmates had escaped. These were some bad guys, with counts of attempted murder, torture, and kidnapping on their rap sheets. And because there are only two body counts at the jail per day, the escapees may have had as much as a fifteen-hour head start.

The sheriff's department has not released all the details of exactly how these three prisoners fashioned their escape. Details of this latest inventive and daring escape are being kept under wraps to avoid copycats. But based on what we know, the fugitives' methods involved either making or smuggling in a pretty elaborate set of tools.

The three men were housed in a large dormitory with sixty other inmates. Near their bunk was a metal ventilation grate that they managed to transform into a doggie door. Once they passed through the grate, they were in the underbelly of the prison, which housed all the plumbing and ventilation piping.

They squeezed and sawed their way over a good stretch of the prison until they eventually worked their way up the piping that took them to the prison roof. There, they cut away extensive barbed wire to finally gain access to the outside.

Finally, they rappelled down five floors with bed sheets that they had fashioned into a rope.

Ironically, their landing point was directly in front of the main entrance. As soon as their feet hit the ground, they were off to the races, no longer prisoners, but living the life of highly wanted fugitives.

When asked about the incident, Assistant Sheriff Steve Kea was quoted in the *Los Angeles Times* as saying, "Never underestimate the ingenuity of inmates with nothing but time on their hands and a grim future behind bars looming ahead. You'd be amazed what they can do."

Now that you're armed with your 3P Key, your call, and your vision, your creative ability to break out of prison will amaze you too.

Jailbreak

Armed with the knowledge of your purpose and your calling, along with a vision of a significant future, you are finally ready for the moment you've been waiting for: taking action. Making it all happen.

It's time for a jailbreak.

Breaking out of jail is a tall order. This is the part of the escape plan where you have to do the hard work of tearing down all the mental limitations and beliefs—the cuffs and shackles—that you identified in chapter 2 as holding you back. You have your 3P Key, your call, and your vision to guide you, so this monumental task can be done. Nevertheless, most of the time, the prisons that have held you hostage for decades are not going to crumble overnight.

Moreover, as we talked about before, a successful jailbreak happens on both sides of the prison wall. You know what success and significance have looked like for you in the past, and you have an idea of what you want it to look like going forward. Now your challenge is to actually build the whole new life and organization you desire, based on your vision for the future.

And let's not forget that you will have to fight resistance every step of the way.

Fear is one of the greatest challenges that lie ahead of you as you undertake your prison break. Every decision to change must pass over the wall of fear in your mind. This means that every opportunity, every change small or large, and every bump in the road will set off the fight-or-flight alarms in your brain. You can't help it. Having this "reptilian brain" around—the part of our brain that ensures that we keep breathing and protects us from any perceived risk to our survival—is just part of being human.

In some ways, that reptilian brain even serves us well. But if you're a leader trying to break out of a mental prison? Not so much.

Even if you personally learn to work around it, that doesn't mean fear is ever going to vanish altogether and let you be. Your reptilian brain will be there on your shoulder with each step you take toward freedom, saying, "For your safety, we will continue to monitor your every movement and will sound the alarm at the first sign of any change you want to make."

Fear is a powerful thing. But do you know what's even stronger?

Your power, your principles, and your purpose. Your calling and your vision. Everything you've worked to excavate in yourself that has brought you to this moment.

Choosing to continue with your jailbreak in the face of fear is making the decision to move forward. And luckily for you, there are additional tools to help you do that.

In this chapter, we will cover how to pick the best path to freedom using a "Possibility Funnel," how to plan the mission that lies ahead for you as a leader, and how to turn your biggest problems into better possibilities by breaking free of "habit handcuffs." These tools will help you finally turn your dream of freedom into a reality.

The Possibility Funnel

Your jailbreak begins with focusing your time and talents on possibilities that have the greatest chance of success. However, figuring out what those are isn't always easy.

You've probably heard the common saying "So many opportunities, so little time." This becomes even truer as you gain clarity through your new lens of what you could do and be in this world. As a leader, you know you have limited capabilities and time—which means you need to have great discernment about where and how you are going to apply your precious resources.

The first step in figuring that out requires taking the possibilities of your vision and running them through what I call the "Possibility Funnel."

How does this funnel work?

CHOOSING THE BEST POSSIBILITY

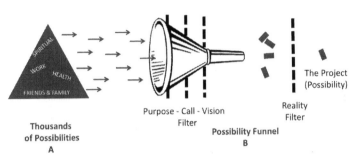

Figure 5.1

First, you have to identify the possibilities that you will feed into your funnel.

In figure 5.1, *A* represents all the new possibilities you can pursue, now that you understand your 3P Key, call, and vision. To identify them, you simply have to give yourself the freedom to imagine what's possible.

This is an opportunity to dream up all the things that *could* happen to move you toward your vision of the future. Do this process in the classic brainstorming fashion, where no idea is a bad idea. Just go for it. Think big. Why not? You're just sitting around in prison anyway, so put your incarceration to good use.

Jot all of your ideas down. Put them in their respective

categories of career, relationships, spirituality, and health. Some ideas may cross multiple categories. Pay special attention to those. If you're like most of the leaders I meet, you'll love the opportunity to address several things simultaneously.

Once you have everything written down, take a few minutes and do a sort. Can some possibilities be combined? Are some ideas unrealistic in the current environment, and should they therefore be moved to a future list? Which possibilities cause the greatest initial excitement for you?

Then, narrow your list down to the top few in each category. These are the possibilities you want to feed into the Possibility Funnel.

In figure 5.1, *B* represents the Possibility Funnel itself. The goal is to feed your best ideas into the funnel to come up with a short list of possibilities—those that will help you create the greatest success and significance for yourself and others.

The funnel has four filters. Take your possibilities and run them through the funnel, in this order:

1. **Purpose Filter:** Rank the possibilities according to how well they align with what you do best. This filter may define what role you should play in the execution of the possibility. For example, if I can be involved in influencing

and getting people on board versus day-to-day execution, that is a much better fit for my skills.

2. **Call Filter:** Does the possibility deliver a direct hit to your call? Does it honor the bull's-eye on the target of what you do? Rank the possibilities accordingly. For example, a possibility that lets you hit your bull's-eye 80 percent of the time gets ranked above one that lets you hit it only 50 percent of the time.

3. **Vision Filter:** Rank the possibilities by which has the greatest potential for delivering on your vision statement. For example, which will affect the greatest number of people while still meeting your criteria of success and significance?

4. **Reality Filter:** How does the possibility fit into the reality of the world at this moment? Is the timing right? Do you currently have the capacity and capabilities to successfully take on this particular possibility? A possibility could rank the highest on the other three filters only to completely fail based on this filter. For example, a person who could be an amazing referral source would like to pursue this

process with me, but for the next six months we are already overbooked.

Rank each of your possibilities from 1 to 10 (low to high) for each filter. Then total the numbers for each possibility and pick the three to five possibilities with the highest scores.

Now compare your finalists. There may be some overriding factors that help you to choose one possibility over another. For example, one of the possibilities may affect fewer people (vision filter) but be more in line with your calling (call filter). In that case, choosing the possibility that allows you to pursue your calling will always bring more personal passion with the potential for greater significance.

At the end of the day, the goal of this exercise is to discover the best path for pursuing your vision. You are looking for the one or two possibilities that have so much power and potential for success and significance that they justify all the resistance you will need to push through in order to break out of jail.

Choose the possibilities that inspire you and allow you to do what you do best. Pick the ones that bolt you out of bed in the morning because the potential is beyond what you have ever experienced before. Once you commit to those, your jailbreak is underway.

The next thing you need is a mission.

Plan Your Mission

Once you have your most promising possibility in your sights, you're ready to transform it from an idea into a reality—and that starts with planning a mission.

A mission is a possibility in action. It is a one-off project you have decided to take on in the pursuit of your vision. Your life is going to consist of hundreds if not thousands of missions that you embark on over time.

Just as you need a compelling vision for the future, each mission demands its own empowering picture of what success and significance will look like when that mission is accomplished.

That's why it's important to take the time to write out everything you hope to accomplish with any given possibility, once you've decided to do it. This is your mission statement (the written form of a mission). Your mission statement should follow these three key guidelines:

- **SCOPE:** The scope of the mission should include everything you desire to achieve for all stakeholders involved, in measurable terms.

- **PLAN:** You should be able to develop a timeline for the effort, describing all of the planned actions, roles, and responsibilities.

- **COST:** Based on the type of mission, there should be a budget. This is the estimated cost to execute and deliver on the goals of the mission.

Every time you complete a mission and realize a possibility, celebrate your accomplishment. Accomplishing a mission means that you are truly living the life of a Jailbreak Leader: you have successfully leaned into your 3P Key, and you have seized a real opportunity to follow your call and create significance—all while bringing yourself one step closer to delivering on your larger vision.

With every mission you complete, you change, becoming more of who you were always called to be. Once you realize a possibility, don't stop there. If you do, only jail awaits. Instead, start the whole process over with a new mission, and a new mission statement.

The more you translate your vision into concrete missions, the faster you'll move toward your goals—and the more successful your jailbreak will be.

Break the Habit Handcuffs

By now, you're on your way. You have the tools to be the best you that you can be. Your vision has shown you where you want to go as you scale the walls and break out of your prison. You have a clear escape plan and a path to get you started on this journey.

With the exception of fear, the single biggest thing that can still throw you right back behind bars is old habits.

Here's how that works. Every prison has routines called "standard operating procedures." These procedures dictate everything that happens in the prison in a highly repeatable way. In other words, where, when, and how an event occurs on a Tuesday at 10:00 a.m. will be exactly the same every Tuesday at 10:00 a.m. The goal is mundane repeatability that provides the same exact result each and every time.

In your personal prison, the standard operating procedures locking you in your cell, day after day, are your habits. The formula looks like this:

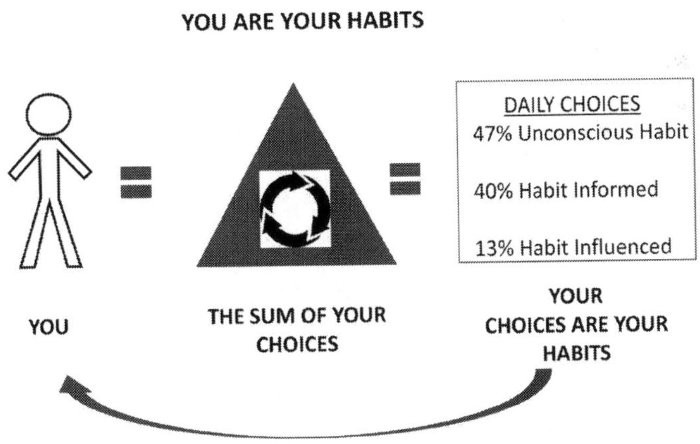

YOU ARE YOUR HABITS

| DAILY CHOICES |
| 47% Unconscious Habit |
| 40% Habit Informed |
| 13% Habit Influenced |

YOU   THE SUM OF YOUR CHOICES   YOUR CHOICES ARE YOUR HABITS

Figure 5.2

For better or worse, the daily ten thousand decisions you've made up to this point in your life have given you the sum result of who you are. You are the sum of your choices, and your choices are influenced by your habits, across the board.

Habits are the processes you unconsciously follow in executing your daily routine. In their book *The Power of Full Engagement*, Jim Loehr and Tony Schwartz state, "We are creatures of habit and as much as 95 percent of what we do occurs automatically."

Now don't get me wrong; habits are necessary and are the natural order of things. According to Loehr and Schwartz, we need to run on autopilot most of the time to conserve our available energy, and that makes sense. Imagine a prison with no standard operating procedures. If the guards had to figure out every single movement of the day from scratch, it would require hundreds of guards and more hours than are available in the day to get the job done. They'd be lucky if they got just one meal organized!

At ground level, you can think of it this way: every morning, you mindlessly get in front of the mirror and go through the exact same ritual of brushing your teeth. And that's a good thing. Anyone who will be within arm's length of you that day will highly appreciate your ongoing brushing habit.

There's no doubt you have hundreds, if not thousands,

of good habits that keep you healthy, safe, socially acceptable, and operating in a fairly positive and efficient manner. But not all habits are good. And when it comes to the ones that are keeping you in jail, there's some good news.

You can break them—and break yourself out of the mental limitations caused by them—by using the change scale.

The Change Scale

No one likes the idea of change. Anyone who says they do either is lying or has never experienced big change.

With that said, change is the ticket to the future you want. And, as shown in figure 5.3, overcoming the resistance to change is like navigating the scales of justice. Until the value of the possibility is significantly greater than all the resistance you're up against, nothing is going to change.

CHANGE SCALE

OVERCOMING THE RESISTANCE TO CHANGE

Figure 5.3

By this point in your jailbreak, however, your possibility does outweigh your resistance. You have the power of your purpose and your calling at your back, and that does a lot to tip the scales. The only thing left to address is that mechanism in the middle: the one labeled "habits."

If you want to do something different in life, you will have to decide which old habits need to go in order to make room for your new vision.

As a very simple example, let's say a particular training program will give you the knowledge you need to keep moving toward your vision, but it's a yearlong course that requires one hour of your time each day. What current activity (habit) are you willing to give up to find that hour of time to participate in the program?

To figure this out, you need to take a look at your current habits. For instance, maybe you watch TV each evening before bed. According to a recent Nielsen report, the average American watches five hours and four minutes of TV every day. (This includes what you watch on your handheld devices.) To make room for your training program, are you willing to trade in an hour of TV every day for an hour of learning?

It sounds simple enough, but most old habits are harder to break than they look. Trading in the mindless fast food of entertainment for actual work may be more difficult than you think. Other tradeoffs you may need to make can include time, money, or even relationships. But one thing is true across the board: when you finally succeed in breaking the habit handcuffs that have been keeping you in jail, the results are always worth it.

Reforming your habits is one of the most powerful things you can do to become a Jailbreak Leader, because it puts you in control of the change scale. That means that you will be able to overcome any kind of change that comes your way—however unpleasant—and keep moving forward in the direction of freedom.

Even better, when you control your habits and the change scale, you gain the ability to make choices that advance your goals. Instead of just being a victim of circumstantial change—the kind that drops on you out of the sky and usually creates major problems at the most inopportune times—you *create* the kinds of changes you know you need to advance your vision. You can even turn circumstantial change into change that works for you.

For example, one of my clients has several offices, and the lease at one of his offices was terminating at the end of the quarter. The landlord announced the rent was going to increase by 50 percent. This was a real-time business problem he needed to address by either accepting the new terms or going through the hassle of relocating.

My client's personal purpose is "Orchestrating Effectiveness." This means he just loves the opportunity to dive into an existing problem and create a highly effective solution. He can see past the existing confusion to how it all can fit together in a harmonious and productive way. One of his passions is to see the local community operate in a more holistic and synergistic way, and he believes the business community can be the driver of that change.

This new circumstance created by the lease issue revealed an opportunity for him to align his purpose with his business and his passion. The year before the landlord's announcement, he had been exploring the concept of a collaborative business model that would align with other strategic companies to help influence the community, while the companies simultaneously continued to grow their businesses. This unexpected facility problem opened the door for him to move to a much larger facility, which he turned into a colocation with his strategic partners.

Because he controlled the change scale, he was able to combine an unexpected circumstance, his call to influence the community, and his unique business philosophy into a purpose-driven outcome. And that, my friends, is how you stage a first-class jailbreak.

Keep Moving

When you make the decision to drive change by choice, circumstantial change will come along for the ride by default. As a leader, you need to make sure these unwanted circumstances don't put you back in prison or knock you off course—and you do that by continuing to move forward with your jailbreak in the face of adversity.

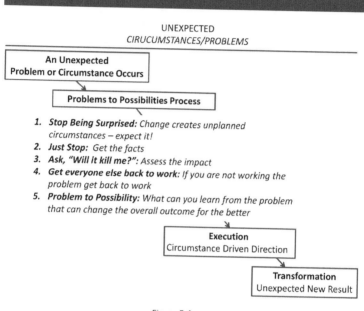

UNEXPECTED
CIRUCUMSTANCES/PROBLEMS

**An Unexpected
Problem or Circumstance Occurs**

Problems to Possibilities Process

1. ***Stop Being Surprised:*** *Change creates unplanned circumstances – expect it!*
2. ***Just Stop:*** *Get the facts*
3. ***Ask, "Will it kill me?":*** *Assess the impact*
4. ***Get everyone else back to work:*** *If you are not working the problem get back to work*
5. ***Problem to Possibility:*** *What can you learn from the problem that can change the overall outcome for the better*

Execution
Circumstance Driven Direction

Transformation
Unexpected New Result

Figure 5.4

Figure 5.4 illustrates a common situation. A random one-off circumstance appears out of nowhere or is directly caused by your efforts to lead a proactive change initiative. In my first book, *Doing the Difficult*, I wrote about the concept of turning problems into possibilities. In the reality of leading change, you're constantly going to be bombarded with the unexpected.

In fact, the bigger the jailbreak you're pursuing, the bigger the problems you should anticipate. In forty years of leading strategic initiatives, I have seen that most leaders, including me, have the exact same response to problems. One, they're always surprised. Two, a huge doom-and-gloom feeling comes over the team, stopping progress in its tracks. Both of these are counterproductive.

When you find yourself up against a tough challenge during your jailbreak, use this five-step process to get things moving again.

1. **Stop being surprised:** You know problems are coming, and as the Jailbreak Leader, you have the opportunity to lead your team through those problems and help them embrace the opportunity for something bigger and better.

2. **Just stop:** Significant problems require an assessment. What's the real issue? Be driven by data and facts, not by stories and rumors.

3. **Ask, "Will it kill me?"** Despite all the alarms going off in your reptilian brain, very rarely does any person, project, or business die as the result of a problem. Put things into their proper perspective.

4. **Get everyone back to work:** Problems in a group environment are like a gnarly car accident. Everyone wants to stop and watch. If

you're not involved in solving the problem, get back to work.

5. **Move from problem to possibility:** Instead of thinking about what you don't want (the problem as described), ask the question "Given the current situation, what do I want?" Run the issue through the Possibility Filter.

   a. Does this new circumstance open a new way to achieve your purpose or enhance the final outcome of your purpose?

   b. What do you now know because of this problem that you didn't know before it occurred?

   c. Given the nature of the problem, do you have your best people (in regard to strengths—not title or function) working on the problem?

   d. Is this problem simply the result of a misguided principle that needs to be adjusted?

For a Jailbreak Leader, a big part of overcoming challenges is recognizing that the most successful projects never end up where they originally intended. You, as the leader, need to hold the end goal lightly and allow the direction of your vision to grow and evolve, based on the latest information.

You and your team are getting more knowledgeable every day. Sometimes, when circumstances hit the fan, they can shake up the way you think and offer huge opportunities to improve your escape plan that you had never thought of before. As a leader, when you learn to embrace these unwanted circumstances for the great potential they may possess, you set yourself up for some of the greatest jailbreaks imaginable.

The Taste of Freedom

How do you know when you've staged a successful jailbreak? What does the freedom of living and leading outside your personal prison actually look like?

- **Personal transformation:** Because the projects you take on are aligned with your power, principles, and purpose, you are forced to use those skills. This no longer happens randomly; it is planned and executed. The more you use your natural skills, the more you will become who you are designed to be.

- **Success and significance:** Your missions deliver on what you have deemed to be most important in the world. You are actively helping to make change in the areas of injustice and frustration you see around you. Success and significance will start to manifest the day you begin a project and will continue to grow from there.

- **Participation of others:** Everyone wants to be aligned and involved with things that matter. No matter what your business, significance is now part of what you do. Those you lead now have the opportunity to engage on a higher level, and as a leader you can also help to bring your team members into alignment with themselves, based on their individual purposes in life. When leaders truly lead, others get to go along for the ride.

- **One step closer:** Every day takes you one step closer to the vision you have created—the ultimate outcome you desire to create in the world.

The Moment of Truth

In chapter 3, I mentioned the movie *The Great Escape.* The POWs who escaped that maximum-security German prison were extraordinary. But here's the flip side of the coin.

Only 76 of the original 250 prisoners who planned to escape made it out that night, thanks to various problems and challenges. The prison held thousands of prisoners, and many more than the original 250 participants were invited to be part of the escape. The sad reality is that a large number of them decided it was better to stay put in their prison cells and wait out the war than to take the risk of breaking free.

At some point, you have to make that same decision. As much as you may realize that the majority of fears and beliefs holding you back are not even true, they still represent a very powerful force. Are your desires for freedom and the value of what you have been called to do great enough to help you overcome the perceived fear and risk of breaking out of jail?

This is an honest question. A friend once told me, "People are too committed to their current situation to change." They have kids to raise, they're not going to walk away from a business they started fifteen years ago, or there's no way their spouse is going to pack up and go on some wild adventure ride. These may be valid considerations for many people. But they are not the call you are being presented with as a Jailbreak Leader.

Your call is to be fully committed to getting started, wherever that starting line may be for you. Pick that one place in your business or relationships where you can begin to pursue your jailbreak. Even if that place is small, commit to it! Sitting on the fence, with one foot dangling over freedom and the other foot stuck in the prison yard, is always the worst place to be at any level of change.

This is your moment of truth.

As you commit to your calling and sprint down the path of your escape, you'll experience a continued personal transformation. Each day you spend operating outside of your old habits and building new ones, fresh possibilities begin to evolve and become part of your normal routine. As the old habits die and the new ones are born, a never-before-seen, optimal version of you is established.

This is your ticket out of your mental prison—the ticket that will finally give you the freedom to lead with purpose. This, at last, is your jailbreak.

But just because you escape from prison once doesn't mean you're home free forever. In the next chapter, I'll show you how to stay outside the system once you've broken loose, so that you can remain a fugitive—living and leading on your terms—for the rest of your life.

Chapter 6

Fugitive

The passionate pursuer has all the earmarks of a fugitive.

—*Eric Hoffer*

Whitey Underground

One of the most notorious individuals to ever evade the reach of the law as a fugitive was James (Whitey) Bulger.

Whitey was a very bad dude. After his arrest, he was arraigned in federal court on July 6, 2011. He pleaded not guilty to forty-eight charges, including nineteen counts of murder, extortion, money laundering, obstruction of justice, perjury, narcotics distribution, and weapons violations.

He was also an ingenious fugitive.

Whitey didn't escape from prison. He leapfrogged directly to fugitive status after being tipped off that the law was coming for him by John Connolly Jr., a retired FBI agent whom Whitey worked with as an informant.

And once he went into hiding, Whitey managed to elude arrest for sixteen years—no easy feat, given that he had a $2 million bounty on his head, second only to Osama Bin Laden. How did he do it?

He did it by transforming himself into someone else.

Whitey and his long-time girlfriend, Catherine Greig, first took up residence as Charlie and Carol Gasko in Santa Monica, California—on the opposite side of the continent from Whitey's stomping grounds in New Jersey. He and Greig underwent considerable plastic surgery. Furthermore, the moniker "Whitey"—a nickname that Bulger despised—had been derived from his shocking white-blond hair. When he was finally taken into custody at the ripe old age of eighty-six, law enforcement found that he had traded in his now gray hair for dyed black hair.

Appearance wasn't the only thing Whitey changed. His Santa Monica neighbors described this hardened murderer and his companion as "just a very nice couple" and said that Whitey was "a very lovely person."

As FBI agent Scott Bakken noted, "To be a successful fugitive, you have to cut all contacts from your previous life." That piece of wisdom gave one of the most wanted criminals in the United States freedom from incarceration for the better part of two decades. It can give you freedom from your mental prison too.

Fugitive

Whitey's case offers us a great look at the extent to which we must go to successfully avoid being pulled back into the mental jail of incarceration. James Bulger evaded the law for as long as he did because of one key thing:

He chose to be different, not better.

The core of Whitey's success as a fugitive was his ability to walk away from the idea of just becoming better at what he already did. Law enforcement knew his MO and was watching all his colleagues. They knew what he liked, where he went, and everything else there was to know about Whitey Bulger.

But they didn't know anything about Charlie and Carol Gasko, "the nice couple living the good life," as described by neighbors. Those neighbors couldn't even imagine Charlie in the persona of a murderer and extortionist. Instead of taking his original skillset and becoming a better and more elusive criminal, Whitey became an entirely different person.

Now that you've escaped from mental prison, you have the opportunity to do the same thing—to transform yourself into someone entirely new and leave the old, imprisoned version of you behind in the dust.

Now a word of warning: this is more challenging than it sounds. Unlike a quick external change such as plastic surgery or coloring your hair, your internal transformation evolves over time. And all the while, obstacles will continue to throw themselves in your way, trying to derail you from your purpose and your calling.

This is truly the hard work of Jailbreak Leadership. But is it worth it?

Absolutely.

One of the toughest charades in life is trying to measure up. The best disguise you will ever have, as a fugitive Jailbreak Leader, is simply being your authentic self. When you embrace that everything about you is 100 percent right for what you are supposed to be doing here, your life begins to flow naturally and becomes deeply satisfying. It was only the jail talk that told you to be something other than what you are in the first place.

Imagine letting go of all of those expectations. That is freedom. And it's only the beginning.

Imagine getting to do what you do really well and love to do, and even being asked to do it by the people around you on a day-to-day basis. Imagine not having to try anymore to fudge your way through tasks you know you're terrible at. That is freedom too.

Imagine being free to give. You do not have to hoard things or talents anymore. You don't have to worry about not having enough. You already have enough. In fact, you have more than enough, and realizing that you live in abundance means that you can freely give value away. You are like the UPS man of life—a conduit for the freedom of others. That is not just freedom—that is freedom on steroids!

All of this can be your reality. But if you're serious about making progress on your journey as a Jailbreak Leader, you'll need to avoid the potential snare of getting re-incarcerated—and that's going to require a couple of tools. This chapter will show you how to keep your purpose at the forefront of your leadership and how to use a "purpose organizer" and outside accountability to keep yourself free of shackles in the long term.

Purpose First

One of the greatest challenges you face, as a fugitive from mental prison, is keeping your purpose at the forefront even after the mundane realities of running an organization from day to day begin to set in again. But when you make it happen, the opportunity speaks for itself.

Compelling data is coming in that demonstrates the power and success of a purpose-led business. Companies that promote sustainability and purpose are quickly becoming winners in the marketplace—in the eyes of both the customer and the employee. The next generation of employees and consumers is already demanding an authentic and compelling purpose beyond what most people have been content for decades to settle for. And that kind of authentic purpose and vision can only come from you, the Jailbreak Leader.

So what can you do to keep your purpose at the forefront of your actions, even when the humdrum tasks of maintaining your business start to weigh you down?

You continue to engage daily with everything you've learned by writing out your 3P Key and your call. Then, as part of a daily planning exercise, you pick the one thing you will do toward advancing your vision.

For my clients, the shift toward putting purpose first is a thirty-day process focused on changing habits, staying in touch with the "why" of what they are doing, and actually taking action to pursue their missions. At the end of the thirty days, assuming all goes well, they have truly owned who they are, made progress toward their short-term goals, and successfully learned how to manage change.

They have shifted into a purpose-first mindset.

For leaders who willingly make the move to put purpose first, the payoff is huge. Not only do you get to lead from your strengths and address the things that you feel are important in your business environment, but you get to do those things for a consumer base that is not just willing, but actually begging to pay for it.

The playing field for purpose-driven organizations is wide open. All you have to do is claim your place on it.

On Parole

Another way to remain a successful fugitive is, ironically, to put yourself on parole.

Convicts often get released early from jail. When that happens, they are assigned a PO, or parole officer. The PO has many roles. One is to be a guide and support for the convict, helping him or her assimilate back into society. The PO is also there to help ensure that newly released convicts are doing what they're supposed to be doing. This includes laying out a plan of action for the convicts and a method for measuring and tracking their progress.

To help ensure your success as a Jailbreak Leader, you're going to be assigned a different kind of PO—a "purpose organizer." You can receive your very own PO at www.jailbreakleadership.com.

Your PO requires five minutes of your time every day. The goals are specific:

- **Review and Remind You of Your 3P Key and Calling.** As the cornerstone of who you are and where you're going, this is a daily reminder of your importance, your contribution, and where you're going.

- **Check In with Your Operations.** Change has no room in the day if operations aren't working well. This is a quick, measurable check to see whether everything is operating smoothly or something needs special attention. Failure of operations is the quickest way back to jail.

- **Identify Your "One Big Thing."** This is the opportunity to select the one thing you'll do today to move your purpose forward. Successful change happens one day and one step at a time. Plan it, schedule it, and protect it.

- **Create Your To-Do List.** This is your well-organized and prioritized action plan for the day. The majority of our time is, and will always be, consumed with the activities of life. Again, change and seizing the opportunity to live your purpose require smooth-running daily operations.

This PO is the same written exercise I use with my clients to help them shift into purpose-driven leadership. They send me their PO worksheet daily, and each week we have an hour-long call to discuss progress. As simple as this sounds, the results experienced by leaders after just thirty days of engaging with their PO are always astounding.

A full set of operating procedures is included with your purpose organizer. And a word to the wise: you don't want to take your parole officer lightly, or you're going to end up right back in jail again. Using your PO is the first new morning habit you must drill into yourself to ensure your success as a fugitive Jailbreak Leader. It is the single most powerful habit you can form to achieve the change you're looking for. Just as in the judicial system, having a PO is not an option!

Partner Up

There's one final tool for remaining a successful fugitive as a Jailbreak Leader: accountability.

Life has a way of consuming you. Changing that is not about discipline; it's about creating structure for yourself through a schedule, and then protecting that schedule.

Accountability helps to reinforce this process. Leaders are people of integrity. While we may let ourselves down sometimes, we rarely let another person down.

As a Jailbreak Leader, enrolling others in your journey creates accountability. Especially when the work you are doing to stay out of mental prison is still at a personal level, having a coach, partner, or someone on a similar journey walking with you can make all the difference between success and re-incarceration. If you find yourself going it alone, we are here to support you. Just drop me an email at info@jailbreakleadership.com.

The life of a fugitive is tough work. Besides dealing with the backward pull of old habits, you have to fight the lure of complacency and the jail alarms of fear that sound every time you attempt to do something different. Those inclinations and alarms are never going to change. However, they will become much easier to deal with if you have someone in your corner who understands, and who can cheer you on through the rough spots. Get some help!

Take It Slow

The path to lasting transformation as a Jailbreak Leader is never a straight line. Even when I look at my own journey over the past several years, I can see how I kept taking one step forward, followed by a three-quarter step back. Instead of becoming a completely new person like Whitey did, I kept defaulting back to what I knew and was comfortable with.

Every time I did, those safe choices threw me right back in jail. Until finally, in 2016, I decided to cut ties with my old way of doing things once and for all.

One of my key contacts at my old, safe organization was astonished by my decision. "How can you be so all in, have the skills, and now just up and leave?" he demanded.

Doesn't that sound exactly like what your friends from the old neighborhood would say?

Embracing your new life as a fugitive means embracing the step-by-step process of transformation that pulls you forward each and every day. You have to stay vigilant about it. The call back to the old ways is very powerful.

But when you can hold your own in the face of the forces trying to pull you back, you gain an irreplaceable reward that was always out of reach for you in prison: freedom. And the taste of freedom is sweeter than that of safety, any day. We'll explore this in the next chapter.

Chapter 7

Freedom

The future depends on what you do today.
—Mahatma Gandhi

The Long Road to Freedom

The 1994 film *The Shawshank Redemption* follows the story of Andy Dufresne—and speaks to every aspect of Jailbreak Leadership.

In the movie, Andy, a young executive for a large bank in New England, is tried and falsely convicted of murdering his wife and her golf-pro lover. He is sentenced to life at Shawshank State Penitentiary.

Over the next twenty years, we follow Andy's difficulties behind bars. He spends extended periods of time in solitary confinement and is subject to repeated rapes, beatings, and even the murder of a fellow inmate who could have identified his wife's actual murderer.

Part of the story is the relationship between Andy and fellow lifer Ellis Boyd "Red" Redding, the prison contraband smuggler. When they first meet, Andy asks Red to get him a rock hammer and a large pinup poster of glamorous actress Rita Hayworth. Not knowing exactly what a rock hammer is, Red gets very inquisitive. "Are you going to use this for a weapon or for tunneling?" he asks Andy. But when the miniature hammer finally arrives and Andy shares his hobby of rock collecting and sculpting with Red, the smuggler is put at ease. "It would take a man forty years to escape with that thing," he says to his delivery guy with a smile.

While on a work detail one day, Andy overhears the brutal captain of the guards, Byron Hadley, complaining about the taxes he is going to have to pay from a recent inheritance. At great risk, not sure how Hadley is going to react, Andy offers his expertise in finance.

After he saves Hadley a large sum of money, Andy's life in prison changes significantly.

Andy gets transferred from his work detail to the library, where he becomes the in-house financial advisor for all the prison staff, including the warden. With Andy's help, Warden Norton begins to scam the prison system, skimming money from the public works program he'd started. To launder the money, Andy creates a fictitious character and opens several bank accounts in the character's name. As Andy shares with Red, "The warden is going to retire a millionaire."

But unbeknownst to us, the viewers, it turns out that throughout this whole movie, Andy has had a very focused purpose.

One morning at roll call, he is gone—just disappeared into the wind. Upon investigation of his cell, a tunnel is discovered, its entrance hidden behind the pinup. Sure enough, Andy had been very busy over the previous twenty years with his rock hammer. He tunneled into the bowels of the prison's plumbing system and, from there, broke into the main sewage line, slogging through five hundred yards of nasty excrement to freedom.

Sporting the warden's suit, the next day Andy shows up at bank after bank and, as the imaginary character he had created, cleans out the warden's accounts. As a transformed and now rich man, he heads off to Mexico to live the rest of his life on his terms—and he never looks back.

Like Andy, many people spend decades incarcerated by the prisons of our minds. You have probably been among them. But now, you have everything you need to stage a jailbreak that can set you on the path to freedom—permanently. And that holds the promise of a future you may never have dreamed of before.

A New Future

You are on the verge of a new future.

The drivers of this new future will be the leaders in the world who are willing to do what it takes to operate outside of the prison system. These are leaders who will make the decision to use their own 3P Keys as the cornerstones of where they are going. In the past, leaders depended on a novel approach or a new technology to make a difference. In this new future, purpose-driven leaders drive change from their core beliefs—from a universal need to fix a wrong in the world.

This approach not only brings them a much greater sense of purpose personally and professionally; it also becomes the call to action for others who want to be part of something bigger than themselves. For this reason, Jailbreak Leaders will give rise to teams that will become potent, effective, and influential forces in the world.

This is the endgame of breaking free of the constraints of our mental prisons, casting an amazing vision of what could be possible for others, and fully working in alignment with who we have been called to be.

This is Jailbreak Leadership. And now, you have everything you need to carry this new way of leading out into the world—and to reap the benefits.

Your Personal Escape Plan

From the day Andy entered the Shawshank Prison, he stuck close to his purpose. He worked with the end in mind. He stayed focused on escape. Everything he did guided and informed that purpose. From the direction of his tunnel, to befriending the warden, to the creation of the fictitious person, to the stockpiling of the money, every move was crafted to create the path to his escape.

He built his escape plan, one careful choice at a time. Now it's time for you to build yours.

Breaking out of prison is no easy task. If the path ahead seems daunting, you don't have to do it alone. A growing community of other leaders seeking to work from their true purpose is available to you—along with a variety of other resources—on the www.jailbreakleadership.com website.

And, as you already know from my purpose, call, and vision for the future, I am dedicated to changing the world through helping leaders lead with purpose. My role is to support your efforts in any way I can, whether that is by speaking to an organization or by connecting with you for a one-on-one jailbreak consultation. Please feel free to reach out to me personally at info@jailbreakleadership.com if I can be of any assistance on your journey.

At Large

Now that you're armed with the tools to break out of prison, you can live, lead, and design a world for yourself that goes far beyond what you ever thought possible when you were locked behind bars.

As a Jailbreak Leader, you have embarked on a lifetime journey. It's the journey of a fugitive, and it's a journey of transformation. Every day, you get to make informed decisions based on being free and leading a purpose-driven life. This calling is not a one-and-done event but a step-by-step process of evolution— one that will create significance and impact both in your life and in the organizations you've been called to lead.

True Jailbreak Leadership is about serving others. It's about the opportunity to show up as the best version of you, delivering on your purpose and using your strengths in everything you do, every single day. Everyone is counting on you to lead the way. We all need you to do what you do!

I hope you are inspired by the rediscovery of what you already knew about yourself, before it slowly slipped away. I hope you embrace the freedom of being you and knowing that you are exactly who you are meant to be. As you embark on your new journey as a Jailbreak Leader, I also wish you great success and significance. May you have a bigger impact on the world than you ever thought possible, and may you inspire those you lead to find and live out their purposes in life as well.

It's time to make your jailbreak. Shed the cuffs and shackles that have bound you your whole life. Run as hard and as fast as you can for freedom—the freedom to live out your purpose, play the game to your strengths, and be the success you've always imagined you could be.

May you never find yourself incarcerated again. And if you do, remember, just like my friends on *COPS*: don't go down without a fight!

ABOUT THE AUTHOR

Jeff Blanton is the founder and CEO of The Blanton Group, an organization dedicated to helping leaders transform purpose into possibility. A highly sought-after speaker, author, and leadership coach, he assists business leaders across the country to make the shift from success to significance.

Prior to founding The Blanton Group, Blanton spent more than thirty years successfully leading large strategic change initiatives for organizations of all sizes, from well-funded start-ups to Fortune 100 companies. These became the backdrop to his understanding of the role a leader must assume in this changing world and the foundation of his powerful Jailbreak Leadership process.

Today, businesses must go beyond the bottom line to thrive. They must also provide social value and create meaning and purpose in society. This can be facilitated only by the authentic personal purposes of those leaders bold enough to take this challenge on. Blanton's mission is to free today's leaders to live out their callings and authentically bring them into the business environment, so that they can change business and society as we know it.

In addition to The Blanton Group, Blanton is a founder of and partner in several consulting companies. He is also involved with multiple local nonprofits and social enterprises focused on effecting positive change in his community. Blanton resides in San Diego, California, the Finest City in America, where he does his part to make that slogan a reality.

Made in the USA
San Bernardino, CA
17 November 2017